Edexcel Economics A
Theme 4: A Global Perspective

By

Brendan Casey

CW00841051

Other titles in this series

Edexcel Economics A
Theme 1: Introduction to Markets and Market Failure
Theme 2: The UK Economy - Performance and Policies
Theme 3: Business Behaviour and the Labour Market

ISBN 978 1535589543

Table of Contents

About the author

The author is Head of Economics at Ashbourne Independent Sixth Form College in London, and is a graduate of the London School of Economics. He has been teaching the Edexcel A level economics syllabus for over 15 years, and has also been an examiner for this syllabus.

Globalisation

1

1.0 Globalisation

1.1 Definition

Globalisation means the increased integration between countries economically, socially and culturally. The World Bank defines it like this: "The growing interdependence of countries resulting from the increased integration of trade, finance, people and ideas in one global market place"

1.2 Characteristics of globalisation

- The rapid expansion of international trade: in 1960 world trade was 10% of world GDP, but by 2010 it was 24% (WTO).
- Global products and services, e.g. Apple, Ford, HSBC.
- Increased capital transfers between countries, e.g. for investment, currency transactions, FDI.
- Growing importance of multi-national companies (MNC's)
- Increasing world economic inter-dependence, e.g. complicated global supply chains - cars, mobile phones.
- Globalisation of technology
- Increased labour migration between countries, e.g. in 2000 175m people lived outside their home country, but by 2013 this had risen to 232 million (UN)

1.3 Factors contributing to globalisation

Reduction in trade barriers - due to agreements arrived at first through GATT (General Agreement on Tariffs and Trade) and now the WTO (World Trade Organisation) trade barriers have been much reduced. This has opened up markets in Asia, Africa and Latin America to the West and vice-versa. This has integrated the economies of countries in difference continents in a way that wasn't possible before.
Growth of trading blocs – the growth of trading blocs such as the EU, NAFTA and APEC has aided the process of globalisation because its opened up new markets for different countries previously separated by trade barriers.

Globalisation

The growth of multi-national companies (MNC's) – MNC's have been able to take advantage of economies of scale and reduced trade barriers to trade on a global scale. In just 30-40 years it's now become normal to see global brands and global products, e.g. Microsoft, ICI, Coca-Cola. MNC's with their factories in one country, and markets in another, have joined together the economies of countries worldwide.

Improvements in technology - improvements in technology have helped globalisation in three ways:

- Cheaper products – improvements in productivity have made manufactured goods more affordable, e.g. cars, TV, DVD's. This has encouraged international trade.
- Communication – it's easier for firms to communicate both internally and externally with other firms and their customers, e.g. fax, telephone, e-mail, video-conferencing. Again this has encouraged international trade and expansion.
- Banking – it's easier for businesses to borrow, lend and send money. This has greatly increased world trade.

Capital mobility - in the 1980's and 1990's many countries abandoned exchange controls and government policies aimed at supporting currencies at particular levels. This has encouraged the free flow of capital around the world and the whole process of international trade.

Decrease in cost of transport - decrease in air, shipping, road and rail costs have made it cheaper to export than ever before. This has encouraged international trade.

Others

- Growth of the Internet
- Single currencies e.g. the euro
- Collapse of the Soviet Union
- Opening up of China
- Deregulation and privatisation of businesses

Evaluation

- Arguably you could say the reduction in trade barriers in the post-war period has been the most important factor contributing to globalisation. Without it we wouldn't have seen the huge increases in world trade, as its made goods cheaper and made it much easier for businesses to trade worldwide. Having said that, in the last 20 years we could say the internet has become the most important factor.

- Globalisation is not a new phenomenon - you could argue it started in the colonial period in the 19th century e.g. British in India. All we are witnessing is an acceleration of the process, not something new.
- Doubts have begun to grow about the benefits of globalisation and there has been a trend recently to talk about its short-comings, e.g. economic interdependence, downward pressure on wages in the West. Some are even now talking about de-globalisation.

1.4 Impact of globalisation on consumers, producers, workers, governments the environment, and countries

(i) Consumers

Advantages

- Lower prices – firms have used economies of scale and cheap labour from developing countries to reduce costs, and then passed this on to consumers reducing prices. The fall in prices has been particularly pronounced in manufactured goods, e.g. computers, TV's, i-pods.
- More consumer choice – because of more trade consumers have had access to a more varied choice of goods. We see this not only with manufactured goods but also with services such as tourism and food.

Disadvantages

- Less consumer choice - globalisation has led to the growth of MNC's and oligopolies. This has squeezed out independent shops and small businesses leading to the 'clone-town' effect we see in countries like the UK with high streets dominated by the big brands.
- Higher prices - you could argue, at times, prices have been too high because globalisation has led to increasing market concentration ratios in different industries, i.e. oligopolies, making it easier for firms to collude.

- Weakening of native cultures – globalisation has led to a homogenised 'world culture' and weakening of distinctive cultural groups. We see this particularly with clothes, food and household goods. Branding and economies of scale now mean that consumers in Beijing do not look much different from consumers in London.

(ii) Producers

Advantages

- Lower costs - firms can maximise their economies of scale and use cheap labour in developing countries to maximise their profits.
- Bigger markets - firms can now sell their products globally and develop global brands increasing revenue and profits, e.g. Toyota, Honda.
- Tax avoidance - big firms have taken advantage of different tax laws in different countries to minimise the tax they pay.

Disadvantages

- Inter-dependent global supply chains - if there is fault in a factory in China, for example, it could effect manufacturers of the final product in Germany. This then has a knock-on effect to profits.
- Tax avoidance - bad publicity could effect sales, and it could get harder in the future, e.g. the OECD has recently proposed new rules to combat it.

(iii) Workers

Advantages

- Higher incomes/more jobs – globalisation has created more demand and therefore more jobs. This has led to rising incomes and rising GDP around the world.
- Reduced absolute poverty in developing countries– globalisation has created more jobs, and better paid jobs, in developing countries reducing absolute poverty rates. We see this particularly with China, India and in Africa.

Globalisation

Disadvantages

- Unemployment and widening income inequalities in Western economies – offshoring has led to de-industrialisation in the West and the loss of many jobs in manufacturing. Some studies also show that globalisation may have led to widening gaps between rich and poor. This is because the remaining Western manufacturers have had to respond to fierce competition from abroad by lowering wages. There is also more competition in the labour market from migrant labour.

(iv) Governments

Advantages

- More growth, more jobs, reduced rates of poverty - globalisation has allowed governments to fulfil many of their economic objectives. This has been particularly true of developing countries, e.g. between 1981-2010 China lifted 680m people out of extreme poverty.
- More tax revenue - this has allowed governments to build infrastructure, schools and hospitals and increase peoples living standards.

Disadvantages

- Unemployment and widening income inequalities in the West
- Tax avoidance from MNC's - the benefit from the increased tax revenues of more growth could have even been greater.
- Low growth, higher inflation in the future - there has recently been a surge in the prices of commodities such as oil and copper, and basic foodstuffs such as rice and wheat. A lot of this has been attributed to China and India's rapid industrialisation. This could lead to a period of lower growth and higher inflation in the future.
- Increased inter-dependence of the world economy - the economic problems of one country can now have effects on other countries in ways it wasn't possible before, e.g. credit crunch 2008.

(v) Environment

Advantages

- Increased living standards and growth have made people around the world more environmentally aware, e.g. Greenpeace, WWF.

Disadvantages

- Globalisation has led to more greenhouse gasses, pollution and soil erosion. This is leading to a legacy that will be difficult for future generations to correct.

(vi) Countries

The syllabus mentions that you should know the impact of globalisation on countries. This is an all-encompassing category, so it includes all the categories above. If you are asked about it say the obvious things about jobs, incomes, growth, tax revenue and the environment

Patterns of trade and terms of trade

2

2.1 Factors influencing the pattern of trade

Comparative advantage - this looks at the impact on trade of the opportunity cost of production. As it changes so will the pattern of trade, e.g. improvement in labour skills, investment. For a full discussion see section 3.2.

Emerging economies - these have greatly effected the pattern of trade in the post-war period, e.g. in 1995 China had 10% of world exports of high-tech goods; by 2014 this had risen to 25% (World Bank). You should also be aware of these terms and acronyms to describe the emerging economies past and present:

- Tiger economies - a small group of countries from SE Asia who have become major exporters of manufactured goods, e.g. Hong Kong, Malaysia, Indonesia.
- BRIC - Brazil, Russia, India, China. Sometimes it's called BRICS; the S is for South Africa.
- MINT - Mexico, Indonesia, Nigeria, and Turkey

Trading blocs and bi-lateral agreements - trading blocs influence patterns of trade because they create free trade areas. This incentivises trade between the countries inside the bloc and disincentivises it outside. Similarly bi-lateral agreements are designed to promote trade between two countries which may be at the expense of others. For a more detailed discussion see section 5.0.

Changes in exchange rates - if the exchange falls against another currency, e.g. pound against the US dollar, it will make exports to that country cheaper and imports more expensive. In this way it will effect the pattern of trade. For more detail see section 9.0.

Others

- Tariff and non-tariff barriers
- FDI
- Changes in relative inflation rates
- Changes in competitiveness, e.g. labour costs

9

2.2 The UK's pattern of trade

There are two features of UK trade you should be aware of:

The UK's share of world manufacturing has been in steady decline – this is true of all the G7 countries in the recent past. The major reason has been cheap labour from China, the Tiger economies and now Eastern Europe and India. This has made the Western economies uncompetitive and so MNC's have switched their manufacturing plants from Europe to Asia and SE Asia.
Major trading partners – the UK's major trading partner is the EU. The EU accounts for about 45% of exports and 55% imports (ONS 2014). The USA is the UK's next major trading partner. It accounts for about 17% of exports and 9% of imports (ONS 2014). The BRIC countries percentage of exports and imports is growing all the time.

2.3 Terms of trade

The terms of trade is the price of exports relative to the price of imports. It's expressed as an index number.

(i) Calculation

$$\text{Terms of trade} = \frac{\text{Index of export prices}}{\text{Index of import prices}} \times 100$$

(ii) Factors influencing a country's terms of trade

- Exchange rate - a fall in the exchange rate makes exports cheaper and imports more expensive worsening the terms of trade.
- Inflation - if inflation rises in a country relative to others it will make exports more expensive improving the terms of trade.
- Productivity - an increase in productivity relative to other countries will make exports cheaper worsening the terms of trade.
- Incomes - the prices of primary products rises less quickly than the prices of manufactured goods and services; that's because they have a lower YED. Therefore, if you are a country relying mainly on the export of primary products, while importing a lot of manufactured goods and services,

over a period of time you will suffer from a declining terms of trade. This is called the Prebisch-Singer hypothesis and often happens to developing countries. See also section 14.6.

- Tariffs - if a country imposes a tariff on imports this will raise import prices and worsen its terms of trade.
- Demand for exports and imports - if there's a change in demand for imports and exports effecting their price this will change the terms of trade.

(iii) Impact of changes in a country's terms of trade

The impact of changes in a country's terms of trade is complex and depends on factors such as:

- PED of imports and exports, e.g. availability of substitutes
- How big the rise/fall in the terms of trade is
- How long rise/fall in terms of trade lasts
- Which goods we talking about - the terms of trade measures a basket of goods but not all goods have the same price increase/decrease.
- What we mean by improvement and deterioration in the terms of trade, e.g. an improvement in the terms of trade could mean export prices have risen or import prices fallen.

Below are stated just two cases; ceteris paribus assumption applies. In the exam you will have to look at each case on its merits.

Improvement

Caused by rising export prices and PED for exports is elastic.

- Living standards - these should improve as it means a country can buy a bigger quantity of imports with the same amount of exports.
- Balance of payments, growth, jobs - if the terms of trade improved this would mean a deterioration in the balance of payments because exports are now more expensive. It would also mean slower growth because AD (AD = C + I + G + X - M) would shift to the left, and a loss of jobs because exports would get less competitive.

11

Deterioration

Caused by rising import prices and PED for imports is elastic.

- Living standards - these should get worse as it means a country can buy a smaller quantity of imports with the same amount of exports.
- Inflation - rising import prices could cause 'imported inflation' because import costs of raw materials would increase causing cost-push inflation. The price of imported finished goods would rise as well, and in a country like the UK with a high marginal propensity to import (MPI) with many of these finished goods included in the CPI, it would add to inflation as well.
- Balance of payments, growth, jobs - rising import prices would mean the balance of payments improves because imports are more expensive so less would be imported. It could also mean an improvement in growth because there would be less leakages in the economy, and more jobs because domestic producers would get more competitive.

Specialisation and trade

3

3.1 Definitions

Absolute advantage – this means a country can produce a good at a lower production cost than another country.
Comparative advantage – this means a country has a lower opportunity cost than another country in producing a good.
Specialisation – the process by which a country develops an expertise in producing a particular good or service.

3.2 Using PPF's to illustrate the difference between absolute and comparative advantage

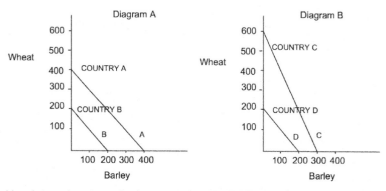

Absolute advantage is demonstrated in PPF diagrams by the PPF of one country being above the PPF of another country, e.g. in Diagram A we can say Country A, has an absolute advantage over Country B in both wheat and barley. Comparative advantage on the other hand is shown by a difference in *gradients*. In Diagram B, we can see that although Country C has an absolute advantage in both goods, Country D has the comparative advantage in barley because its opportunity cost ratio for barley compared to wheat is 1:1, whereas for Country C its 2:1. Where gradients for both countries are the same no country has a comparative advantage, e.g. Diagram A.

3.3. Absolute advantage and trade

Specialisation and trade

Adam Smith (1723-1790) said there would gains to trade for countries if they specialised in the goods in which they had an absolute advantage. We can see this in the example below, assuming that each country can produce the following amounts of output devoting half of their resources to wheat and half to barley.

Without specialisation

	Wheat	Barley
Country A	500	2000
Country B	1500	400
Total	2000	2400

Clearly country A has the absolute advantage in barley but country B has the absolute advantage in wheat. If they now specialise this will be the production pattern:

With specialisation

	Wheat	Barley
Country A	---	4000
Country B	3000	--
Total	3000	4000

If each country now trades half their surplus with the other country we can see both will be better off than their initial position:

	Wheat	Barley
Country A	750	3000
Country B	2250	1000
Total	3000	4000

Notice this is also better for world output as it creates more growth, jobs and incomes.

3.4 Comparative advantage and trade

David Ricardo (1772-1823) took Adam Smith's work one stage further and said that there would be gains to trade for countries if

Specialisation and trade

they specialise or partially specialise in the goods in which they have a lower opportunity cost. This is known as the theory of comparative advantage; see below. We again assume that these are the production patterns for two countries devoting half their resources to each product.

	Cars	Wheat
Country A	2000	2000
Country B	500	1000
Total	2500	3000

At first sight we might think there will be no gains to trade for Country A from trading with Country B, as it has an absolute advantage in both products. However, using the theory of comparative advantage we can see that there is. Country A has the comparative advantage in cars, but Country B has the comparative advantage in wheat: the opportunity cost for country A is 1 car but for country B it's 0.5 cars. If Country A now partially specialises in cars and Country B completely specialises in wheat we can see there is an overall gain from trade of 500 cars:

	Cars	Wheat
Country A	3000	1000
Country B	---	2000
Total	3000	3000

If Countries A and B now trade their surpluses, e.g. Country B trades 1000 wheat for 750 cars, both will be better off.

3.5 Assumptions/limitations of theory of comparative advantage

- Ignores transport costs
- Ignores external costs
- Ignores economies of scale – assumes constant production costs
- Assumes perfect factor mobility
- Assumes perfect knowledge - buyers and sellers
- Assumes goods are homogeneous

3.6 Advantages and disadvantages of specialisation and trade

Specialisation and trade

Advantages

- Higher world output, growth and jobs
- Higher living standards
- Lower prices, more choice for consumers
- Economies of scale for producers, e.g. purchasing economies, technical economies
- Innovation - free trade implies competition, this should lead to market innovation and higher quality goods.

Disadvantages

- Overdependence/increase in risk - some countries can become dependent on the export of one or two goods, e.g. oil, copper, coffee. A lack of diversification can leave the economy vulnerable to falls in demand.
- Income inequalities - for countries specialising in primary commodities it will mean incomes of workers don't rise as fast as for countries specialising in manufactured goods. That's because there's a difference in the YED's.
- Unemployment - trade implies competition, if one country specialises in the production of a good it will put other less efficient firms in other countries out of business.
- Strategic vulnerability - a country could become too dependent on other countries for strategically important goods, e.g. food.

Trade liberalisation

4

Trade liberalisation (free trade) means reducing trade barriers between countries and promoting free trade, i.e. getting rid of tariffs and quotas. Initially the negotiations were done through GATT, now they are being done through the WTO.

4.1 Advantages of trade liberalisation

(i) For consumers

Lower prices – more competition on an international level means firms have to compete harder on price. Larger markets also mean firms can maximise economies of scale and therefore reduce prices.
More choice – more competition means firms have to offer a better choice to win customers.

(ii) For producers

Access to larger markets – increased trade means higher revenues and profits for businesses. It also means they can get better economies of scale and reduce costs.
Access to cheaper sources of raw materials – therefore they can cut their costs and increase their profit margins.

(iii) For the government/economy

Higher economic growth - it creates more opportunities for exports and if it creates more jobs they'll be more spending and investment in the economy.
More jobs – more trade and more output means more jobs are created.
Higher incomes - more jobs and more export opportunities for firms ought to lead to higher paying jobs.
Reduced balance of payments deficit - since it should lead to more exports.

4.2 Disadvantages of trade liberalisation

Free trade tends to benefit developed countries – their firms are bigger and more powerful, e.g. Ford, Toyota, and can take advantage of the dismantling of trade barriers, whereas the poorer countries can't. The gap between the two gets bigger not smaller.

Higher unemployment – for those people working in industries that were previously protected there may be job losses, e.g. UK - steel industry 2016.

Over specialisation – countries may over specialise. This could make their economies more vulnerable to sudden changes in demand.

May encourage dumping – countries that produce large surpluses may try to dump them on world markets at low prices. This could create unemployment for marginal producers in other countries, e.g. Chinese dumping of steel in 2016

Strategic problems – too much specialisation may mean that countries under-produce goods that are of strategic significance and this gives them problems in the long run, e.g. food, arms.

Problems for infant industries – the dismantling of trade barriers may mean infant industries come under too strong competition. This could affect growth and jobs in the long run.

External costs – higher world growth leads to more pollution and greenhouse gasses. It also means the loss of non-renewable resources such as oil and gas.

Protectionism

5

Protectionism means the policies used by countries to erect barriers to trade e.g. tariffs, quotas.

5.1 Methods of protection

Tariffs (import duties) – this is a tax imposed on imported goods. The advantage is that it can be used to raise tax revenue; the disadvantage is that it could produce shortages.

Quotas – these are restrictions on the quantity of imports into a country. A disadvantage over tariffs is that it doesn't raise any tax revenue.

Non-tariff barriers – these are barriers which don't involve taxing imports, e.g. bureaucracy, technical standards. They reduce imports because it makes it more complicated for an exporter to get their goods into another country. Countries often favour this method because it's difficult to prove.

Subsidies to home producers – this means giving grants to domestic producers to lower their production costs, e.g. the Common Agricultural Policy (CAP) of the EU.

5.2 Graph

Tariffs

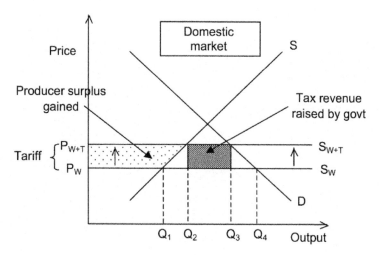

Protectionism

Key

P_W = World price
S_W = World supply without tariff
P_{W+T} = World price + tariff
S_{W+T} = World supply + tariff
Q_1 = Domestic supply before tariff
Q_2 = Domestic supply after tariff
$Q_1 \rightarrow Q_4$ = Imports before tariff
$Q_2 \rightarrow Q_3$ = Imports after tariff

Initially domestic supply will be Q_1 and the volume of imports will be Q_1 to Q_4. After the imposition of the tariff, domestic production will expand to Q_2 and the volume of imports will fall to Q_2 to Q_3. The net result is that some domestic producers get protected, Q_1 to Q_2. However, consumers lose out because consumer surplus is lost and they have to pay higher prices.

5.3 Arguments for protectionism

To protect jobs - there may be a lot of pressure on the government in certain industries to protect jobs. Protectionism can also be used to ease the pain of structural unemployment, e.g. deindustrialisation in the UK in the 1970's.
To reduce a balance of payments deficit – protectionism reduces imports; therefore it reduces a balance of payments deficit.
To protect infant industries - some businesses can be of long term benefit to the economy providing jobs, growth and exports. If they are not protected in the early years they might die out before they bear fruit, e.g. the new hi-tech businesses encouraged by the government in the 1970's.
To prevent dumping - protectionism prevents other countries from dumping their surpluses on your country. Dumping can cause unemployment and damage the long-term health of an industry.
To avoid over specialisation - protectionism can ensure a country has a better spread of industries. This means it is better able to survive changes in world demand.
Strategic reasons - protectionism can mean a country has a minimum level of production in strategically important goods, e.g. food, arms, energy.

Short-term breathing space for run-down industries – protectionism can give an industry a breathing space so the firms in it can re-invest and modernise and become internationally competitive again. Once they've done that the government can remove the protection.

Economies of scale – home firms can take advantage of the protection to expand output and get economies of scale. Once they are competing on an equal footing with foreign companies the protection can be removed.

To raise tax revenue - for developing countries tariffs could be an important source of tax revenue.

5.4 Arguments against protectionism

Lack of competition and build up of monopolies - protectionism reduces competition. This means that domestic businesses may build up monopoly positions, which are bad for consumers. Another problem is there is less incentive for businesses to become more efficient leading to a waste of resources.

Reduced consumer choice - lack of competition from imports means reduced consumer choice. Domestic businesses don't have the incentive to be innovative and consumers are denied access to foreign products.

Higher prices - without competition, businesses can raise prices more easily. This means higher prices for consumers and can lead to inflation.

Retaliation - if one country imposes trade barriers, others will usually retaliate. If this happens there may be a drop in world trade and nobody benefits.

Unfair competition – protectionism means that a country has an unfair advantage, e.g. subsidies to home producers.

5.5 Impact of protectionism on world trade – a practical example

A good example of protectionism is the Common Agricultural Policy (CAP) of the EU. This uses a combination of tariffs, subsidies and guaranteed minimum prices to protect EU farmers. The impacts have been as below. Many of these points can be used in other cases, e.g. textiles, steel or tin.

Surpluses and dumping – guaranteed minimum prices and export subsidies have encouraged EU farmers to overproduce and dump their surpluses. This has then created unemployment and falls in income in other countries.

Inefficient use of resources – the CAP has meant that world resources haven't been being used in the most efficient way. Inefficient farmers in the EU have stayed in business and consumers have been paying too much for their food.

Trade conflicts – arguments about the CAP and dumping have often led to retaliation and a contraction in trade with other countries involving other goods. This has benefited no one.

Trade diversion – protectionism has given the EU countries an incentive to do more food trade with each other. The lack of tariff barriers and a common external tariff has made it cheaper. This has diverted food trade away from their old trading partners and created unemployment in their farming industries instead.

Trading blocs and the role of the WTO

6

6.1 Trading blocs

A trading bloc is a group of countries that have agreed to have a free trade area with each other. There are four types:

Customs union – this is a group of countries which agree to have free trade with each other but impose a common external tariff (CET) on imports from other countries, e.g. EU.
Free trade area – this is a group of countries which agree to have free trade among themselves but retain separate trade barriers against other countries, e.g. NAFTA.
Common market - this is a customs union where there is freedom of movement of both labour and capital. There are also product standards and laws governing freedom of movement of goods and services, e.g. EU, Mercosur, West African Common Market.
Monetary union - this is a group of countries that share a common currency, e.g. eurozone

6.2 Regional trade agreements and bi-lateral trade agreements

Regional trade agreements - these are trade agreements between at least two parties to reduce trade barriers among themselves They include free trade areas and customs unions, e.g. EU, NAFTA.
Bi-lateral trade agreements - these are agreements between two countries or two trading blocs to reduce trade barriers between themselves.

6.3 Trade creation and trade diversion

Trade creation – this means firms within a trading bloc taking advantage of the lack of trade barriers to expand output and find new markets within the trading bloc countries.
Trade diversion – this is the shift in trade that takes place once a trading bloc has been created. A lack of trade barriers and/or a common external tariff creates an incentive for the member countries to do more trade with each other and less with their old trading partners. The shift in trade is called trade diversion.

6.4 Advantages and disadvantages of regional trade agreements (RTA's)

Advantages

- Trade creation - they create more trade between the countries inside the trading bloc. This should create more jobs and growth.
- More FDI - MNC's are more likely to invest in the free trade area they can avoid tariffs and other trade restrictions.

Disadvantages

- Trade diversion - trade is diverted away from former trading partners outside the bloc, e.g. when the UK joined the EU it began doing less trade with the Commonwealth countries. This could effect their jobs and growth.
- Country may be better off outside trading bloc - a country may be better off signing lots of bi-lateral agreements with other countries, rather than being part of a group arrangement. This was one of the arguments behind Brexit.
- RTA's can leave developing countries worse off - e.g. an RTA between the EU and a developing country, or group of developing countries, is likely to open up their markets to significantly more imports.
- Less efficient use of world resources - trading blocs distort comparative advantage because they entail the use of trade restrictions.

6.5 Conditions necessary for the success of a monetary union

Bear in mind that a monetary union means a central bank and a one size fits all monetary policy, e.g. in the eurozone there is the European Central Bank (ECB) and all member countries have the same interest rate. It also means maintaining fiscal discipline, so there are effects on fiscal policy too, e.g. in the eurozone, budget deficits can't be more than 3% of GDP or a country is fined. This is part of what's called the Fiscal Compact (2012).

There are four factors which are often cited; it's referred to as Optimum Currency Area (OCA) theory.

Mobility of factors of production, e.g. labour - if there is mobility of labour then the problem of having the same interest rate for every country will be minimised. If there are economic shocks, like a recession in one country, then the workers there can migrate to another country where there are more jobs. The usual policy response of adjusting interest rates downwards in the country with the problem won't be necessary.

Price and wage flexibility - if these are flexible it diminishes the need for exchange rate adjustments to regain competitiveness. Having the same currency becomes less of a problem.

Fiscal integration - some form of automatic fiscal transfer system is needed for countries which are doing badly, e.g. Greece, Portugal. This will remove the need for exchange rate adjustment which might have been the normal policy response. Again, it minimises the potential problems of having a single currency.

Countries need to have similar trade cycles - if they are different in different countries it means interest rates could be appropriate in one country but not in another.

Others

- Similarity in inflation rates
- Financial markets integration
- Political integration.

6.6 Advantages and disadvantages of a monetary union

A monetary union falls into the definition of an RTA but is analysed and evaluated separately for simplicity. The best example of a monetary union is of course the euro.

Advantages

- Savings on transaction costs - there is no need to convert currencies. This saves businesses time and money
- Planning and budgeting - a single currency eliminates the uncertainty and risk of exchange rate fluctuations. It makes it easier for businesses to plan and budget ahead; this encourages more businesses to participate in trade leading to higher economic growth.
- Lower prices and lower inflation - a single currency means consumers can compare prices more easily. It puts

pressure on producers to keep prices down and therefore should reduce inflation.

- Increased foreign investment - a single currency encourages more FDI because firms don't have to worry about changing from one currency to another and don't have to worry about fluctuations in the exchange rate. This should create more jobs and growth.

Disadvantages

- Loss of control of monetary policy – this could lead to macro-economic problems for individual countries in the monetary union in the long-run because they can't change their interest rates according to local conditions, e.g. inflation, unemployment, growth.
- Reduced control over fiscal policy – members of a monetary union have to maintain fiscal discipline, e.g. in the eurozone they can't have budget deficits higher than 3% or they will be fined. It therefore limits the amount of borrowing a government can do in order to control the economy. Like the loss of monetary policy this could create macro-economic problems for individual countries in the future because it limits their ability to adapt government borrowing according to local conditions, e.g. during a recession.
- Loss of exchange rate flexibility – countries lose the advantage of having different exchange rates against different countries both inside and outside the monetary union.

6.7 The role of the World Trade Organisation (WTO)

The WTO has three main functions:

- To reduce trade barriers and promote free trade
- To resolve trade disputes
- To provide a system of trade rules

The idea is that free trade promotes world growth, a more efficient use of world resources and benefits everyone. Each set of talks between trade ministers is called a 'round' and there have been nine rounds of talks so far. The last one was called the Doha round and started in 2001. Negotiations broke down in 2008 but still haven't resumed.

6.8 Possible conflicts between RTA's and the WTO

The trend towards bi-lateralism and regionalism in trade comes into conflict with the WTO, because the WTO is trying to promote free trade between all members. Clearly bi-lateral agreements and RTA's go against this.

It tries to get around this by negotiating tariffs down, and of course it acts as the arbiter when trade disputes arise. The average tariff between WTO members is now about 9% (WTO 2013), although there are variations between goods

International competitiveness

7

<u>7.1 Definition</u>

International competitiveness means the competitiveness of a country's exports abroad and its ability to compete with imports at home. It will depend on price and non-price factors such as, quality, reliability and brand name.

<u>7.2 Measures of international competitiveness</u>

The main measures are:

- Relative unit labour costs
- Relative export prices

<u>Others</u>

- Productivity
- Unit costs
- Levels of investment
- Research and development (R&D) expenditure
- Training and education

<u>7.3 Global Competitiveness Index (GCI)</u>

This is a composite index produced by the World Economic Forum. It's made of what's called the twelve pillars of competitiveness. These include health and education, efficiency of goods and labour markets, development of financial markets, infrastructure and technology. The top ten rankings in 2015-16 were:

1. Switzerland	6. Japan
2. Singapore	7. Hong Kong
3. USA	8. Finland
4. Germany	9. Sweden
5. Netherlands	10. United Kingdom

<u>7.4 Factors affecting international competitiveness</u>

This is similar to the list above:

Productivity – the higher the productivity the lower will be the labour cost per unit. This means a country's goods will be more price competitive.

Quality and reliability of products – the higher the quality of the goods the easier it is to sell them. Nobody wants poorly made products.

Investment – the higher the level of investment the more competitive the products will be because it will reduce production costs.

Training and level of qualifications of the workforce – a well-trained workforce is a productive workforce and will lower production costs.

Exchange rate – a falling exchange rate means exports get cheaper and imports more expensive; a rising exchange rate means imports are cheaper and exports more expensive.

Quality of management – highly skilled managers can reduce production costs and come up with new ideas that make firms more competitive.

Marketing – advertising, branding, image and reputation all affect sales. The more expert is the marketing the more competitive the products will be.

Macro-economic stability - e.g. low inflation, low unemployment. This creates the right climate for investment and expansion.

Government policies - e.g. taxes, benefits, interest rate. These affect incentives to work and start your own business. Where incentives are high it will increase international competitiveness.

Ease of raising finance – where it's easy to raise finance it increases investment and risk taking and so increases international competitiveness.

Innovation (R&D) – the invention of new products increases international competitiveness because it means new markets can be found and patents can be taken out to protect those markets.

Others

- Unit costs
- Entrepreneurship
- ICT skills

7.5 Benefits and problems of international competitiveness

Benefits

International competitiveness

- Current account surplus
- Lower unemployment
- Higher economic growth - AD will be shifting to the right because exports will rise and imports fall.
- Rising incomes - rising standards of living
- Greater tax revenue - government has more to spend on merit goods, reducing income inequalities and improving infrastructure.

Problems

- Rise in the exchange rate - this would decrease international competitiveness in the long run.
- Retaliation - one country's surplus is another country's deficit. Deficit countries might bring in tariffs and other forms of protection leading to trade wars. There might also be currency wars as other countries try to restore competitiveness.
- Inflation - large volumes of exports will shift AD to the right and could increase inflation. The extra demand for factors of production, like land and labour, as the economy expands could also push their price up causing cost-push inflation.

7.6 Government policies to improve international competitiveness

(i) Cuts in income tax

Advantages

- Increases incentive to work – therefore raises productivity and lowers per unit costs.
- Encourages entrepreneurship and innovation – makes it worthwhile for people to start their own business.

Disadvantages

- Might cause income inequalities to rise.

Loss of tax revenue – this might mean less government spending on public services like health and education. This could affect international competitiveness in the long run.

(ii) Cuts in corporation tax

International competitiveness

Advantages

- Leaves more profit left over for investment – therefore firms can go out and buy latest technology and improve productivity.
- Leaves more profit over for training – this could improve productivity.
- Encourages entrepreneurship and innovation – it's more worthwhile to start your own business.

Disadvantages

- Extra profits may be used to reward shareholders with bigger dividends not for investment.
- Business confidence may be low so firms don't go out and invest, e.g. recession, slow growth.
- Less tax revenue for government – therefore public services, e.g. health, education may deteriorate and it could have a negative effect on international competitiveness in the long run.

(iii) Cuts in unemployment benefit

Advantages

- Increases incentive to work – therefore raises productivity.
- Government has more money to spend on infrastructure and helping exporters.

Disadvantages

- Might cause income inequalities to rise.
- Workers need to have jobs to go to
- May de-motivate the unemployed – therefore they give up on the idea of working altogether and productivity falls.

(iv) Incentives for investment, e.g. tax breaks on capital investment

Advantages

- Encourages firms to invest more – therefore they can raise productivity, lower per unit costs and become more competitive.
- Encourages firms to be more innovative and go out and buy the latest technology.

Disadvantages

- Less tax revenue for the government to spend on public services, e.g. education, health therefore international competitiveness decreases in the long run.
- Business confidence may be low so firms don't go out and invest, e.g. recession, slow growth.
- Investment may not be done wisely – it could be wasted on the wrong type of capital equipment, therefore productivity doesn't really improve.

(v) Education and training

Advantages

- Raises productivity and creates a more highly skilled workforce.
- Helps to fill skills gaps.
- Reduces the amount being spent on unemployment benefit – therefore there is more money left over for improving public services.
- Increases long-term competitiveness.

Disadvantages

- Cost – taxes may have to rise to pay for it.
- Quality – have to make sure money isn't wasted on poor quality training courses.
- Time lag – may take a long time to work.

(vi) Privatisation

Advantages

- Private sector may increase efficiency making the industry more internationally competitive, e.g. BT, BP.

- Less government money needs to be spent on subsidising state owned industries – therefore more money is left over for other public services.
- Government may be able to reduce taxation – therefore indirectly increases incentive to work.

Disadvantages

- Most privatisations have been done in the UK – there's not much left to privatise.
- Privatisation may result in private sector monopolies if not properly regulated – therefore consumers lose out.
- Privatisation may not increase efficiency – if a privatised company has a dominant position they don't have an incentive to improve.
- Privatisation may result in more externalities, e.g. accidents - railways.

(vii) Others

- Improve infrastructure
- Remove regulations, e.g. health and safety, employment protection, environment.
- Devalue the exchange rate - this is only open to those countries operating a fixed or managed exchange rate system (see section 9.2). It wouldn't be open to the UK and other Western economies because they operate a floating exchange rate system.

7.7 Measures which firms could take to improve international competitiveness

Improve productivity - this could be done by increasing investment and training. This would reduce per unit costs and make the firm more price competitive.
Improve the quality of the product - e.g. design, features, brand name.
Rationalisation - this means cutting costs by eliminating waste and duplication, e.g.

- Closing down unprofitable factories
- Shifting production to one or two main sites to maximise economies of scale.

Relocate production abroad - e.g. China, S.E. Asia – in order to take advantage of cheap labour and cut costs.
Switch to overseas suppliers – firms could switch suppliers to cut costs.
Improve overseas promotion - e.g. attend trade fairs.
Go for the top-end of the market – here competition may be less and consumers are less concerned about the price.

Others

- Pricing strategies, e.g. discounting, under-cutting rivals, limit pricing
- Improve customer service

7.8 The UK's recent export performance

The UK's exports have been in steady decline for a number of years. There have been periods of recovery and stability but the overall picture has been a steady downward trend. A number of factors have contributed to this:

- Competition from China and S.E. Asia - UK firms haven't been able to compete with their cheap labour costs.
- A lack of investment & training – this has meant productivity has been lower than our competitors and therefore costs have been higher.
- Failure of the government to support exporters, e.g. through subsidies or management of the exchange rate.
- Quality and reliability of UK exports - hasn't been good enough to compete in world markets.

Balance of payments

8

8.1 Definition

The balance of payments is the sum total of a country's income and expenditure on foreign trade together with all its international capital movements. It's split into two sections - the current account, and the capital and financial account.

8.2 Current account

The current account shows trade in goods and services. It also shows income from employment and investments from abroad; and transfers which have been made by governments and individuals. There are two different types of imports/exports – visibles and invisibles:

Visible imports / exports – these are goods that you can see, touch and feel, e.g. cars, manufactured goods, oil.
Invisible imports/ exports – this is trade in services or income and profits from foreign subsidiaries, e.g. insurance, tourism, shipping, profits from foreign subsidiaries, dividends.

When exports are bigger than imports it's called a surplus, when imports are bigger than exports it's called a deficit.

8.3 Capital and financial account

This records capital inflows and outflows. It's made up of three types of transactions – direct capital investment including FDI, portfolio investment in stocks/shares and bonds, and lastly banking flows ("hot money"). The balance on the capital and financial account should be equal and opposite to the current account balance, so the balance of payments always balances. In reality the capital and financial account always contains a 'balancing item', which represents errors and omissions in the figures.

Examples of capital inflows/outflows are below:

Capital inflow - e.g. a Japanese company investing in a car manufacturing plant in the UK (FDI); a foreign bank making a loan to a UK company.
Capital outflow - e.g. a UK company investing abroad; a UK bank making a loan to a foreign company.

8.4 Causes of a balance of payments deficit

Lack of competitiveness – e.g. quality, cost, design, lack of investment, training.
Inflation – inflation may be higher than in other countries therefore costs and prices are higher.
Exchange rate – may be too high therefore exports are more expensive.
Trade cycle - the balance of payments is cyclical. For countries such as the UK, which have a high marginal propensity to import (MPI), when there is a boom it tends to move into deficit, but when there is a recession it moves into a slight surplus. This is because during the boom employment levels are high and incomes are rising sucking in imports, but when there's a recession spending falls and so spending on imports fall as well.
Government policies – for example:

- Monetary policy – interest rates may be set high to control inflation but this also raises the exchange rate making exports more expensive.
- Supply-side policy – not enough being done to improve training.
- Fiscal policy – taxes too high decreasing incentives to work and invest.

8.5 Causes of a balance of payments surplus

Very competitive economy - e.g. high productivity, investment, training, quality
Inflation - lower than other countries so costs and prices lower
Exchange rate - low, so gives country a competitive edge
Natural resources - some countries have large natural resources, but small populations. It's relatively easy for them to run a trade surplus, e.g. Kuwait, Norway.
Trade cycle - one country's deficit is another country's surplus. For very competitive economies, or economies which have valuable commodities like oil, when there is boom in the world economy

they will have a trade surplus, but when there is a slump their trade surplus will go down.

Government policies - the government will be making the right decisions to keep the economy competitive, e.g. low interest rates, low taxes, investment in infrastructure.

8.6 Problems of having a large deficit

It may signal a long-term loss of competitiveness – this could result in lower living standards in the long run as there may be fewer jobs and lower incomes.

It may mean higher unemployment – a trade deficit means that imports are higher than exports and therefore jobs could be lost in manufacturing.

It may mean higher inflation – a trade deficit could lead to a falling exchange rate. That would mean import costs would go up causing imported inflation.

Fall in GDP – a balance of payments deficit is a withdrawal from the circular flow of income. Therefore, it causes a fall in growth.

It may mean an increase in government borrowing – in a fixed exchange rate system it means the government might need to borrow more to support the exchange rate. This could affect public spending and public services in the long run, e.g. education, health.

Evaluation

- It depends on how big the deficit is and how long it persists - e.g. the balance of payments is cyclical therefore it may not be a cause for concern.
- It depends on whether there is a surplus on the trade in services to balance it out – for example this often happens in the UK.
- It depends on what the imports are - if they are mainly of capital goods, and therefore for investment, this may improve the long-term competitiveness of the economy and reverse the deficit in the future.
- It depends on whether the government is pursuing a fixed or floating rate exchange rate policy – if it's floating a balance of payments deficit should be self-correcting.
- Under a fixed exchange rate policy it depends whether the government has previously accumulated budget surpluses – therefore it doesn't need to borrow to finance a deficit.

Balance of payments

8.7 Problems of having a large surplus

Retaliation – one country's surplus is another country's deficit. Countries with large deficits may retaliate by putting up trade barriers to reduce imports. This could result in a trade war and less trade in the future.

Rise in the exchange rate – this could make exports more uncompetitive in the long run and encourage cheap foreign imports.

Inflation – large volumes of exports could increase inflation.

8.8 Policies to correct a balance of payments deficit

(i) Fiscal policy – raise income tax

This is known as a deflationary policy because it deflates the economy. Consumers will have less disposable income so they will spend less and therefore imports will be reduced. For countries such as the UK with a high marginal propensity to import (MPI) it should be particularly effective.

Evaluation

- Unemployment and lower growth – reducing consumption could lead to a fall in demand for domestic goods as well. Firms may react by making workers redundant to cut costs and this could lead to a negative multiplier effect.
- Falling business confidence and investment – reducing consumption could lead to falling business confidence and investment. This could make the UK less competitive in the long run.

(ii) Monetary policy – raise interest rates

This is another type of deflationary policy. Increased interest rates will reduce consumption because it makes it more expensive to borrow on credit cards and loans. This should mean spending on imports decreases helping to reduce the balance of payments deficit.

Evaluation

- Unemployment and lower growth
- Falling business confidence and investment
- Imports might increase – raising the interest rate will probably increase the exchange rate making imports cheaper and exports more expensive. It could therefore make the situation worse.

(iii) Monetary policy - reduce the interest rate

This would lower the exchange rate and make exports cheaper and imports more expensive.

Evaluation

- Could be a danger of imported inflation because import costs will rise
- May suck in even more imports – lower interest rates makes borrowing cheaper and means consumers have more disposable income because their mortgages are cheaper. This could mean even more is spent on imports and cancels out the affect on exports.
- May have an adverse affect on the housing market – makes mortgages cheaper therefore could create a housing boom. Later on this could create inflation because of the wealth affect

(iv) Supply side policies

This includes policies such as:

- Cutting taxes
- Cutting benefits
- Improving education and training
- Privatisation
- Reducing union power

The idea is to incentivise the workforce to work harder and raise productivity. In this way per unit costs will fall and increase exports. It will also mean home firms can compete better against cheap foreign imports. We have seen how to analyse these in Theme 2.

Evaluation

- Cutting taxes and benefits – may lead to widening income differentials between rich and poor.
- Improving education and training – this depends on the quality of the training and it also raises the issue of funding. Will taxes need to be raised to pay for it? Finally there is a time lag so it would take time to work.
- Privatisation and reducing union power – to a large extent this has now been done in the UK so there is not much left to do. This is more a policy of the past then the future.

(v) Protectionism

This would mean the use of tariff and/or quota restrictions to reduce imports

Evaluation

- It goes against current economic thinking - therefore it's very unlikely to be used. The world consensus is free trade at the moment not protectionism.
- Retaliation – it could result in trade wars and a reduction in trade in the long run.

(vi) Exchange rate adjustment

This would mean reducing the exchange rate to make exports cheaper and imports more expensive. It only applies to countries pursuing a fixed or managed exchange rate policy, so wouldn't apply to the UK or other Western economies because they have a floating rate system (see section 9.2).

Evaluation

- Imported inflation – devaluation pushes up the cost of imports, this could lead to imported inflation in the long run. It could also cancel out the advantage of cheaper exports if the cost of imported raw materials forms a significant part of the final cost of those exports.
- Time lags – it takes time to work. It takes time for consumers to change their behaviour and it takes time for exporters to invest and train up workers to take advantage of increased demand.

- Marshall-Lerner condition – this states that a devaluation will only correct a balance of payments deficit if the sum of the elasticities of demand for imports and exports is greater than one. If the PED of exports is inelastic a devaluation may actually increase the deficit.

8.9 Recent trends in the UK balance of payments

There are three trends you should be aware of:

The balance of trade has been negative – this reflects the general decline in UK manufacturing and increasing competitiveness from abroad, e.g. S.E. Asia, China.
The balance of invisible trade has been positive – this reflects the strength of the UK in services like tourism, finance and shipping. The UK also benefits from investments abroad. About 30% of invisible exports come from the repatriated profits and dividends of UK companies overseas, e.g. ICI, BP.
The current account has tended to move from surplus to deficit in a cyclical manner – when there has been a boom it's been in deficit but when there has been a recession it's moved back to a slight surplus. This is because during a boom people tend to spend more on imports because incomes are rising and employment levels are relatively high. However, during a recession people cut back on spending and so spending on imports falls.

Exchange rates

9

9.1 Definitions

Exchange rate – this means the value of one currency in terms of another currency. It's also known as the nominal exchange rate.
Effective exchange rate – this is also known as the trade weighted index. It measures the value of a currency as a weighted average against the currencies of a country's major trading partners. The weights are proportional to the amount of trade involved. For the UK the major weights would be given to the euro, the dollar and the yen. A base year is selected and the weighted average initially starts at 100.
Real exchange rate – this the exchange rate of a currency adjusted for the relative inflation rates between one country and another. A base year is selected and it initially starts off at 100.

9.2 Types of exchange rate system

Floating – this means the exchange rate is determined by market forces and there is no interference by the government or central bank. All of the Western economies use a floating rate system.
Fixed - this is where the government or central bank sets the exchange rate at a particular level for different currencies. Market forces are not involved. It's also known as currency peg, e.g. Saudi riyal against US dollar
Managed - this is where market forces determine the exchange rate, but the central bank intervenes from time to time to influence its level, e.g. Chinese renminbi. It's also known as a dirty float.

9.3 Appreciation, revaluation, depreciation, devaluation, hot money

Appreciation – this means a rise in the exchange rate in a floating rate system.
Revaluation - this means the government increasing the exchange rate in a fixed rate system.
Depreciation – this means a fall in the exchange rate in a floating rate system.
Devaluation – this means the government decreasing the exchange rate in a fixed rate system.

42

Exchange rates

Hot money – this refers to the short-term speculative flows of money between foreign exchanges in order to make a profit by buying and selling a currency or by taking advantage of differences in interest rates to increase returns on deposits.

9.4 Factors affecting the exchange rate

As with any other commodity exchange rates are determined by the interaction of supply and demand.

(i) Factors affecting demand

Demand for exports - exports have to be paid for in home currency, therefore if exports increase demand for sterling will increase and shift the demand curve to the right. This will increase the exchange rate. See below:

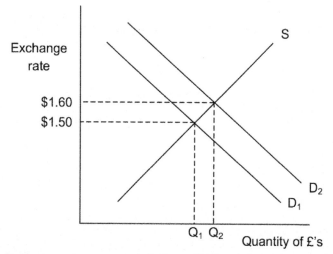

Inflation - an increase in inflation will increase the price of exports and therefore demand for exports will fall. This will shift the demand curve to the left and decrease the exchange rate. See below:

Exchange rates

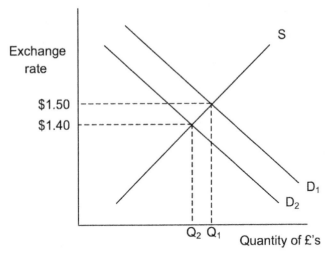

Foreign direct investment (FDI) - if more foreign companies invest in the UK this will increase the demand for sterling. This will shift the demand curve for sterling to the right and increase the exchange rate.

Relative interest rates - a rise in the interest rate relative to other countries will make it more attractive for foreign investors to have sterling deposits (hot money). This will shift the demand curve for sterling to the right and increase the exchange rate. A decrease in the interest rate relative to other countries will have the opposite effect.

Speculation - speculation by large investment funds betting that they can make a large profit on either the rise or fall in sterling will affect the exchange rate.

Strength of the economy (GDP) – growth prospects affect sentiment toward a currency. If GDP is growing relative to other countries then demand for sterling will increase and the exchange rate will rise. If it's falling demand for sterling will fall and so will the exchange rate.

(ii) Factors affecting the supply of a currency

Demand for imports - imports have to be paid for in foreign currency, therefore if demand for imports increases sterling has to be sold to pay for it. This will increase the supply of sterling and shift the supply to the right causing the exchange rate to fall. See below:

Exchange rates

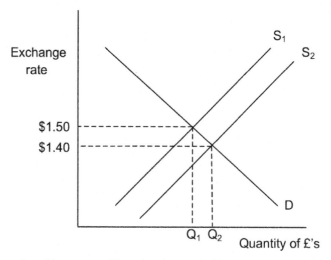

Levels of income - if income levels fall the demand for imports will fall. This will decrease the supply of sterling and shift the supply curve to the left. Hence, the exchange rate will rise.

9.5 Case study in factors affecting the exchange rate

Sometimes in the exam you are required to comment on the factors affecting an exchange rate in the current world economy. Here is an example:

Between May 2007 and November 2008 the exchange rate of sterling against the euro fell from about £1= €1.45 to about £1= €1.20. What were the factors which accounted for this?

UK growth was forecast to fall – this had two affects. First, it decreased sentiment towards the pound. Secondly, it meant that investors expected interest rates to fall because it thought the government would use monetary policy to stimulate the economy. Hot money flows therefore dried up because investors thought they would get a better return on their money with other currencies. The decrease in demand for the pound led to a decrease in the exchange rate.

Falling interest rates – the predictions of slower economic growth came true and UK interest rates fell sharply by about 0.75%. As noted above this made the pound a less attractive currency to hold deposits in because returns were lower.

Housing crash – predictions of a housing crash decreased sentiment towards the pound. A housing crash would mean lower consumer spending (wealth effect) and slower economic growth.
Balance of payments – a widening trade gap put downward pressure on the pound. A rise in imports meant an increase in supply of sterling causing the exchange rate to fall.
Strength of the euro – during this period the outlook for the euro zone was good compared to many other parts of the world. Some predicted that the euro was going to take over from the dollar as the world's dominant currency. This strengthened sentiment to the euro and increased its value.

9.6 Government intervention in currency markets

In fixed and managed exchange rate systems there are various ways a government can intervene to meet its objectives:

- Foreign currency transactions - this means the government, via the central bank, buying and selling it's own currency to engineer increases and decreases in its value. To increase its value it would buy it, to decrease its value it would sell it. It does this using foreign currency reserves.
- Changing the interest rate - this influences hot money flows: if the central bank raises the interest rate it will push the exchange rate up because speculators and deposit holders will get a better return on their money. Decreasing it has the opposite effect.
- Competitive devaluation/depreciation - the government might do this because it wants to make its economy, in particular exports, more competitive, e.g. the Chinese renminbi against the US dollar. The downside is that it can create imported inflation, and retaliation from other countries creating "currency wars".

9.7 Importance of the exchange rate to the economy

The exchange rate is important to the economy because it effects nearly all of the governments' economic objectives. The main points to remember are discussed below.

(i) Balance of payments

Exchange rates

A depreciation or devaluation in a currency ought to improve the balance of payments because it makes exports cheaper and imports more expensive; if it rose the opposite would happen. However, we need to take into account three factors:

Time lags – it takes time for it to work. Firms are committed in the short-term to existing contracts and consumers take time to adjust their behaviour. In the short –run therefore the situation may get worse not better. This is called the J-curve effect:

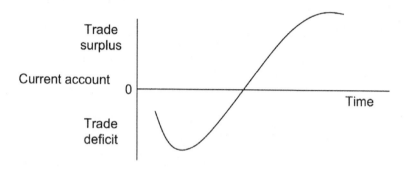

The Marshall-Lerner condition – this states that a devaluation or depreciation in the currency will only correct a balance of payments deficit if the sum of the elasticities of demand for imports and exports is greater than one. If it's not it could make the situation worse not better.

Spare capacity - firms must have the spare capacity to be able take advantage of the situation. If not it will take them time to make investments and gear capacity up.

(ii) Economic growth and employment/unemployment

A fall in the value of the currency would be good for growth and employment because it would make exports cheaper and imports more expensive. This should shift AD to the right increasing economic growth, and create more jobs reducing unemployment. A rise in the currency would have the opposite effect.

(iii) Inflation

A fall in the value of the currency would increase inflation because it would shift AD to the right because exports get cheaper and imports more expensive. It could also cause "imported inflation" because it would make the cost of imported raw materials more expensive creating cost-push inflation. The cost imported finished goods would also rise and because many of these are included on a country's CPI this would raise inflation as well.

A rise in the value of a currency would have the opposite effect.

(iv) FDI

A fall in the value of a currency should lead to more FDI flows because it becomes cheaper to invest in that country, e.g. takeover costs of domestic firms; land costs; purchase of plant and machinery. It would also make exports from that country cheaper, so if the intention is to use that country as an export base that will also increase the incentive to invest.

A rise in the value of a currency will have the opposite effect.

European Union

10

Formerly known as the European Community it originally only had 6 members. By 1986 it had 12 members, now it has 27 members including many of what used to be the Eastern bloc countries.

10.1 European monetary union

This means the adoption of the euro as the single currency of the EU by the EU member states in January 2002. There are three aspects to it:

- A single currency – the euro.
- A central European bank (ECB) – this has the sole right to issue notes and coins. It also sets interest rates for the whole euro zone area.
- Centralised monetary policy – the ECB controls the money supply and interest rate for the whole euro zone. Individual governments have lost their control over monetary policy.

For the advantages and disadvantages of being part of the euro see section 6.6.

10.2 Economic effects if, and when, the UK withdraws from the EU

This is much in the news because of Brexit. The UK still hasn't formally left, but the expected leaving date is 2019:

Change in pattern of trade – reduced trade with other EU countries and more trade with non-EU countries. However, in practice this probably wouldn't happen because the UK is an important trading partner for the EU and special arrangements are likely to be made, e.g. the UK stays part of EFTA.
Unemployment – because exports would fall. This depends on the ability of the UK to develop new markets, e.g. BRIC countries
FDI – this could decrease because firms exporting from the UK to EU countries would now have to pay the CET. However, the flexibility of the labour market could be more important than being part of the EU or euro.
Agriculture – should mean lower food prices because the UK would no longer be part of the CAP. However, this depends on

who the new trading partners are and the stability of world food prices.

Public finances – may improve because the UK no longer has to make it's yearly contribution of about £9bn. However, if unemployment increases it might mean public finances get worse.

<u>10.3 Arguments for and against the UK leaving the EU</u>

The main arguments are these:

For

- **It would reduce government spending** – and therefore improve the budget deficit. The UK's contribution to EU finances is about £9bn per annum. This is money we could badly do with at the moment.
- **Some countries have thrived outside the EU** – e.g. Norway, Switzerland. They have remained part of EFTA, and so have access to the single market, but they are not bound by EU laws on agriculture and fisheries, and can negotiate their own separate trade agreements.
- **It would create a mini-jobs boom** – some euro-sceptics say that red tape on small and medium sized businesses add to costs and prevent firms taking on new workers. They say leaving could create 1m new jobs.
- **UK would be free to establish bi-lateral trade agreements with the BRIC countries** – this would make up for any loss in exports by leaving the EU and in any case this is where world growth is coming from. In the long-run this could be better for jobs and growth.

Against

- **The UK's contribution to the EU is money well spent** – because it helps to build infrastructure in the weaker EU countries who we can trade with in the long-run and so provides jobs and growth for the UK economy.
- **The EU is the UK's biggest export market** – we can't assume that we would be allowed to stay part of EFTA. It could mean hundreds of thousands of jobs being lost, and both growth and the balance of payments would also be negatively impacted.

- **UK firms would have to pay the CET** – this will effect jobs, growth and firm's profits.
- **UK would lose influence over how EU rules are formed** – Norway and Switzerland may be part of EFTA but they can't influence how EU rules are formed and impact businesses, e.g. health and safety, employment laws, financial transaction tax for banks. That will affect jobs and growth in the long run.

10.4 ECB's monetary policy compared to the MPC

ECB's inflation target is a ceiling – the ECB has an inflation target of 'less than 2% over the medium term' while the MPC has an inflation target which is symmetrical, i.e. they have to keep to it within ± 1%.

ECB inflation target is inherently deflationary – this is because it's a ceiling. The MPC's target is not because there is an upper and lower limit. Therefore, it's recognising the dangers of both inflation and deflation.

MPC's target is more flexible – this is because its ± 1% not just a set figure.

MPC's target is revised every year – this again gives it more flexibility compared the ECB.

Inward investment (FDI) by MNC's

11

11.1 Definition

An MNC is a firm that has its headquarters in one country but has its manufacturing and assembly plants in other countries, e.g. BP, ICI, Microsoft, Colgate-Palmolive.

11.2 Reasons for becoming an MNC

Avoid protectionist policies - this means policies such as tariffs and quota restrictions. This reduces costs and increases profits.
Exploit the cheapest costs of production - for example an MNC can use labour from China and raw materials from Indonesia. Again, this reduces costs and increases profits.
Economies of scale - bigger markets mean that costs can be spread over a larger number of units. This improves profitability and competitiveness.
Globalisation - because of globalisation it makes sense to locate manufacturing plants closer to new and developing markets because it reduces the transport costs.

11.3 Advantages and disadvantages to countries of MNC's

We need to bear in mind here, that MNC's invest in both developed and developing countries.

Advantages

- **Balance of payments** - exports of MNC's count as the home country's exports. Therefore it improves a country's balance of payments.
- **Employment** - MNC's provide jobs and training for local workers. This improves a country's human capital and competitiveness.
- **Improves economic growth** (GDP) - MNC's improve the productiveness of the economy. They provide income for workers and investment, which creates a multiplier effect across the economy.

- **Technology transfer** - MNC's introduce new technology and management methods into a country. In the long run this should improve the skill level of the local population.
- **Increase in tax revenue** - from corporation tax on profits, income tax on employment, and VAT on goods and services because more people have more money to spend.

Disadvantages

- **Balance of payments** - MNC's import components from abroad and also send profits and dividends back to their home countries. In the long run therefore the balance of payments may get worse not better.
- **Exploitation of the local workforce** - MNC's may exploit the local workforce with low wages and long hours. In developed countries there is employment protection and unions, but in developing countries this is much weaker so MNC's can exploit the workforce more. Having said this, in the UK there has been a lot of disquiet recently about zero hours contracts and the health and safety practices of some MNC's, e.g. Amazon.
- **Increase in economic growth mainly local** - MNC's do improve economic growth but much of this is regional and local. Only the parts of the country getting the investment really prosper.
- **Externalities** e.g. pollution, safety - MNC's are often accused of a lack of responsibility when it comes to safety and pollution. In developed countries there is legislation controlling externalities, but MNC's try to get around this by lobbying politicians to water down any new legislation that could come into force. In developing countries it's easier for them to exploit the situation because legislation is weaker and the countries really need the investment.
- **Skill level may not improve** - in developing countries the management and technical jobs usually go to foreign workers but the local workers only do the manual jobs. Because of this the skill level of the local workers doesn't improve that much. It's not so big a problem in developed countries because the skill level is higher.
- **Tax avoidance** - because of tax avoidance many MNC's pay very little corporation tax, e.g. Amazon only paid £11.9m of tax in the UK in 2015; UNCTAD estimates the

total tax revenue lost to developing countries as a result of tax avoidance by MNC's was $100bn in 2015.

11.4 Measures to control MNC's

Regulation of transfer pricing - transfer pricing means manipulating prices charged between the separate entities within the MNC, in such a way, that it makes low profits appear in countries with high corporation tax and high profits appear in countries with low corporation tax. This is very difficult to control without an international agreement, because each country is in competition with the others for investment. Also, some countries have begun to specialise as "tax havens", e.g. Luxembourg, Switzerland, Ireland, so are reluctant to agree to it.
Limits to government ability to control MNC's - this is difficult because much is at stake from the investment, e.g. jobs, growth, technology transfer. However, many countries, particularly in the West, have laws supporting employment and environmental protection, so their worst excesses can be controlled. There are also trade unions. In developing countries it's much easier for MNC's to exploit the situation.

Public spending and taxation

12

Public spending means government spending on public goods and merit goods, e.g.

- Health
- Education
- Housing
- Transport
- Social security

The largest single item of public spending is on social security, e.g. job seekers allowance, child benefit and pensions. It accounts for about 35% of public spending. Health and education are the next biggest items, accounting for about 12-15% of public spending each.

12.1 Reasons for taxation

- To pay for government spending, e.g. public goods, merit goods, benefits.
- To reduce consumption/production where there are negative externalities e.g. tobacco, alcohol.
- To provide goods where there are positive externalities, e.g. health, education
- To manage the economy as a whole, e.g. tax rates have an important impact on growth, unemployment and inflation.
- To redistribute income, e.g. tax and benefit policies, provision of merit goods.

12.2 Distinction between capital expenditure, current expenditure and transfer payments

Capital expenditure - this is government spending on long-term investments, e.g. schools, hospitals, roads
Current expenditure - this is day-to-day government spending on goods and services, e.g. salaries of teachers, hospital equipment.

Transfer payments - these are mainly welfare payments to individuals to reduce gaps between rich and poor, e.g. pensions, JSA, housing benefit.

12.3 Reasons for changing size and composition of public expenditure in a global context

Trade cycle - during a recession you'd expect public spending to increase because more has to spent on transfer payments and also the government might bring forward spending on capital projects, like building roads or schools, to keep the economy afloat. During a boom you'd expect it go down as unemployment falls.

Demographics - for countries with ageing populations you'd expect spending on health care and pensions to increase. For those with younger populations it will be a lot less, e.g. Europe vs. Africa.

Economic development - developing countries are a lot poorer than developed ones, and there are problems with collecting taxes and corruption. Therefore, you'd expect public spending to be a lot less in developing countries because they don't have the same tax revenue. Also, in developed countries people are accustomed to high quality public services, which are expensive, and create high expectations.

State of public services - public services, e.g. schools, hospitals, may be run down and in a poor state, so the government needs to update them and spend money on them.

Ideology/politics – in Europe countries favour a mixed economy, in America people favour a free market economy, so you'd expect government spending to be higher as percentage of GDP, e.g. in 2013 government spending was 39% of GDP in America, but in the UK it was 45%, and Denmark 56% (OECD). Denmark has a Gini coefficient of only 0.25 (2012) and is committed to promoting an equal society.

Others

- Immigration
- External shocks, e.g. financial crisis
- Debt interest, e.g. Greece - means less can be spent on public services

12.4 The significance of differing levels of public expenditure as a proportion of GDP

(i) Productivity and growth

You would expect these to rise as public spending increases as it would effect health, education and infrastructure, and therefore improve productivity. It would also shift AD and AS to the right increasing economic growth; there would also be a multiplier effect from its injection. The opposite would be true of a decrease in public spending.

Having said this, one has to take into account evaluation points such as size, quality and incentives. A rise in public spending may be caused by an increase in transfer payments, which could have a disincentive effect.

(ii) Living standards

You would also expect these to rise as public spending rises, because there should be job creation from an increase in government capital spending, and an improvement in schools, hospitals and housing. The opposite would be true if public spending fell.

Having said this, again, a lot depends on what it's being spent on and how effective it is. There may be crowding out for example, and waste, when public spending rises.

(iii) Crowding out

Higher public spending can cause two types of crowding out in the private sector:

- Resource crowding out - this means the shortage in resources, e.g. capital, labour and raw materials, that is created as a result of too much government spending on capital projects, such as building schools and hospitals. It deprives the private sector of those resources and drives their price up, e.g. wage costs.
- Financial crowding out - this means the increase in borrowing costs, as a result of more government borrowing, to fund higher government spending. It raises

interest rates for the private sector because there is more competition for funds.
Lower government spending would ease any problems from crowding out.

(iv) Level of taxation

If public spending is low you would expect taxes to be low and vice-versa. Taxes are the source of revenue for the government spending.

(v) Equality

If public spending were to rise, we might expect equality to improve, because it would mean more job creation from government spending on capital projects such as infrastructure, higher transfer payments and better schools and hospitals. If it were to fall we would expect the opposite.

Having said this, we have to take into account the size of government spending, what exactly it's spent on and incentive effects, i.e. taxes and benefits.

12.5 Types of tax

Direct taxes – these are taxes paid from an individuals or organisation's income e.g. income tax, corporation tax.
Indirect taxes – these are taxes paid on goods and services, e.g. VAT, customs duty.
Progressive taxes – these are taxes, which take a higher proportion of an individual's income the more that individual earns, e.g. income tax.
Regressive taxes – these are taxes, which take a smaller proportion of an individual's income the more that individual earns, e.g. VAT. VAT is regressive because the poor spend nearly everything they earn. Therefore in proportionate terms they pay more VAT than the rich.
Windfall taxes – these are "one-off" taxes on excessive company profits. Usually they are only applied to the newly privatised companies e.g. oil, gas. This is because they may have been able to take advantage of their monopoly position to make bumper profits, e.g. the very high oil price in 2008 ($140 per barrel)

Public spending and taxation

12.6 Economic effects of changes in direct and indirect taxes

(i) Incentives to work

Direct taxes

If direct taxes such as income tax and corporation tax were to rise we'd expect this to have a disincentive effect. Workers would keep less of their pay, and entrepreneurs would keep less of their profits. If income tax went down, however, we'd expect the incentives to rise and more people to come off benefits and seek work, for example.

Indirect taxes

The effect of indirect taxes on work incentives is less clear. Some economists would say a rise in VAT would decrease the incentive to work as each pound you earn now buys less, others that it increases the incentive to work because if you want to maintain your living standard you have to work harder.

(ii) Tax revenue and the Laffer curve

Direct taxes

The Laffer curve shows the relationship between tax revenue and tax rates. See below:

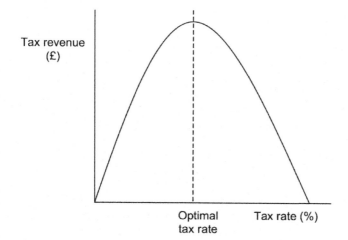

It demonstrates that there is an optimal tax rate and that governments have to carefully weigh up the pros and cons of setting the tax rate at a particular level. If it's too high it could disincentivise the workforce; if it's too low it means they could be collecting more tax if they wanted to. Another reason why increasing tax rates cause falling tax revenue is because it increases tax evasion (illegal) and tax avoidance (legal). This happens for both income tax and corporation tax, e.g. the recent well publicised tax avoidance cases of Starbucks, Google and Amazon.

Indirect taxes

These follow the Laffer curve effect; there's an optimal tax rate, e.g. if a government raises duty on cigarettes and alcohol too much it encourages smuggling or the black market and tax revenue falls.

(iii) Income distribution

Direct Taxes

If income tax and corporation tax were to rise it should make income distribution more even as there would be more money available for transfer payments. On the other hand, we could also say it effects incentives so the effect is not certain.

If we look at income purely in terms of disposable income, then an increase in the higher rate of tax, all things being equal, will make income distribution more even because the higher rate tax payer pays it, but the lower rate tax payer does not.

Indirect taxes

Indirect taxes are regressive, so an increase in them is likely to make income distribution less equal.

(iv) Real output, employment, price level

Direct taxes

If income tax and corporation tax were to fall this should increase output, employment and the price level. Consumption would increase because disposable incomes would rise, and business investment would increase because firms can keep more of their profits. Both of these would shift AD to the right, creating growth and jobs, but also pushing up the price level.

AS would also increase and shift to the right because of the increasing investment; this will cancel out the price increase, above, a certain amount.

If direct taxes rose the opposite should happen.

Indirect taxes

A rise in indirect taxes makes goods more expensive, so there's a fall in consumption. This will tend to decrease growth and employment. The effect on the price level is more uncertain; the indirect taxes make goods more expensive but its offset to a degree but a fall in AD.

<u>(v) Trade balance</u>

Direct taxes

A decrease in income tax should increase the trade deficit. This is because it will increase disposable incomes and therefore consumption of imports. This is particularly true of countries with a high marginal propensity to import (MPI) like the UK.

Indirect taxes

VAT can effect invisible exports like tourism. The British Hospitality Association has recently called for VAT on accommodation and tourist attractions to be cut from 20% to 5% as a way of reducing the UK's trade deficit.

<u>(vi) FDI flows</u>

Direct taxes

Higher income tax and corporation tax rates would act as a disincentive for MNC's to invest in a country. Higher corporation tax would mean they keep less of their profits, and higher income tax might mean it's more difficult for them recruit the best senior staff. They would look to work in other countries where the rewards were greater.

Indirect taxes

Higher indirect taxes might discourage investment by MNC's. It would decrease the purchasing power of consumers in the country they invest in, and make their product more expensive. However, if the product is mainly for export it may not be a problem.

12.7 Automatic fiscal stabilisers and discretionary fiscal policy

Automatic fiscal stabilisers – these are fiscal policies that automatically reduce fluctuations in the trade cycle. For example, spending on unemployment benefit automatically rises during a recession and means that a degree of spending power is retained in the economy. Income tax receipts automatically rise during a boom therefore taking heat out the economy and moderate inflation.
Discretionary fiscal policy – deliberate alteration of government spending or taxation by the government.

12.8 Budget surpluses, budget deficits and national debt

Budget surplus – this means that government tax receipts exceed government spending.
Budget deficit – this means that government spending exceeds government tax receipts.
National debt – this is the accumulation of budget deficits over the years.

The official name for the budget deficit in the UK is the Public Sector Net Cash Requirement (PSNCR). It used to be called the Public Sector Borrowing Requirement (PSBR).

12.9 Structural and cyclical deficits

Structural deficit - this is the budget deficit adjusted for the effect of the trade cycle.
Cyclical deficit - this is the amount of the budget deficit due to the trade cycle.

The structural deficit plus the cyclical deficit equals the total budget deficit. There can also be structural surpluses and cyclical surpluses.

12.10 Factors influencing the size of fiscal deficits

Trade cycle – during a recession budget deficits generally occur because tax receipts are falling and benefit payments are rising. Tax receipts are falling because of rising unemployment and falling company profits; benefit payments are increasing because of rising unemployment. During a recovery or boom the opposite happens and a surplus generally appears.

Demographics - an ageing population means more spending on healthcare and pensions. It also means falling tax receipts because less people are working. In these circumstances you'd expect budget deficits to appear. This is becoming a significant problem for many Western economies because of falling birth rates, e.g. 26% of the Japanese population is now 65 and over; in the UK it's 18% (World Bank 2016).

State of public services - public services, e.g. schools, hospitals, may be run down and in a poor state, so the government needs to update them and spend money on them.

Political factors – there may be popular demand to increase public spending, e.g. to stimulate the economy. Therefore, the government responds by bringing forward infrastructure projects in order to create jobs and a multiplier effect.

Others

- External shocks, e.g. financial crisis
- Debt interest, e.g. Greece, Portugal, Spain - the increase in the size of the national debt has led to an increase in the size of the fiscal deficit.

12.11 Factors influencing the size of national debts

Fiscal deficits or surpluses - if there are persistent fiscal deficits, then the national debt will increase; if there is a fiscal surplus then the national debt will decrease.

Other factors influencing the size of national debts have already been described above in 12.10.

- Demographics
- State of public services
- Political factors
- External shocks, e.g. financial crisis
- Debt interest

12.12 Problems of a high national debt

- May have to raise taxes later to pay it off - this would slow down economic growth in the future.
- May have to make government spending cuts to pay it off - this would effect the quality of public services and the amount that could be spent on benefits.
- Loss of credit rating, e.g. UK is AAA - this could lead to higher interest rates generally, effecting mortgage payments and consumption as well as investment.
- Interest payments – there's an opportunity cost in servicing the debt, e.g. UK debt interest was £35bn in 2015, about the same as the defence budget. In some cases the interest payments are so high a country may have a problem paying off the capital.
- Crowding out - it may mean too many resources are being diverted to government sector projects, such as building schools and hospitals thus depriving the private sector of labour, capital and raw materials (resource crowding out). This increase in demand for factors of production may mean higher borrowing costs (financial crowding out) and higher wage costs for the private sector.
- May be inflationary - an increase in government spending pushes AD to the right increasing inflation.

Evaluation

- Higher national debt may only be cyclical rather than structural - may be due to recession, rather than an underlying problem. When there is a recovery in the economy it could go down again.
- Interest rates on gilts are very low at the moment, so this is less of a problem, and you could argue it's the right time to borrow.
- Unlikely to be inflationary at the moment as growth is slow and business and consumer confidence low.

Public spending and taxation

- Sometimes government borrowing and spending is necessary to keep the economy afloat. Could argue this is one of those moments.

12.13 Ways of reducing a budget deficit

(a) Fiscal policies

(i) Increase income tax, e.g. top rate of tax from 45% to 50%

The top rate of tax could be increased and therefore tax revenues would rise decreasing the budget deficit.

Evaluation

- It could disincentivise the most productive workers and therefore lead to a fall in growth over all, e.g. they might be more reluctant to seek promotion.
- It could affect entrepreneurship and innovation as SME owners will keep less of their money.
- May just increase tax evasion and avoidance so tax revenues don't really increase
- Top 1% of workers already pay 28% of income tax (IFS 2016) so could say they pay their fair share already.
- May deter FDI and so effect jobs and growth. Top companies more reluctant to come to UK as top executives will be less incentivised.

(ii) Increase corporation tax

This would increase tax receipts decreasing the budget deficit.

Evaluation

- Could lead to less investment and growth because businesses are keeping less of their profits. This would effect international competitiveness in the LR.
- Could deter foreign investment (FDI) and so effect jobs and growth.
- May just increase tax evasion and avoidance so tax revenues don't really increase, e.g. Amazon only paid £11.9m of corporation tax in 2015.
- Could effect entrepreneurship and innovation.

(iii) Increase VAT

VAT increased from 17.5% to 20% in 2011. This could be increased again. Some people favour this over increasing income tax, as it's a tax on consumption rather than earnings, so it's discretionary. You only pay more by buying more. It doesn't have the same sort of impact on incentives and productivity as increasing income tax.

Evaluation

- It's regressive - it effects the poor more than the rich. Having said this, the government can get around this by having tax exemptions, reduced rates and zero rates for staple products, e.g. bread, milk.
- Could reduce consumer spending and therefore have a multiplier effect on jobs and growth.
- Could increase inflation

(iv) Reduce government spending, e.g. on benefits, health and education

The aim would be to reduce government spending to reduce the deficit.

Evaluation

- Cutbacks in health and education could affect productivity and the long-term competitiveness of the economy.
- Reducing benefits would widen gaps between rich and poor.

(v) Increase stealth taxes

Stealth taxes are taxes that people don't normally think about and so don't usually notice, e.g. council tax, duty on petrol, stamp duty on house purchases, tax on dividends

Evaluation

- More likely to be accepted by voters
- May just increase tax evasion and avoidance

(b) Monetary policy – decrease interest rates

This would increase consumption and create a multiplier effect. It would also encourage business investment. The net result should be that the economy grows and tax receipts rise, and transfer payments fall.

Evaluation

- Business confidence and consumer confidence may be low so doesn't really increase consumption and investment.
- Might create inflation – therefore it works in the short run but makes the situation worse in the long run.
- Could cause the exchange rate to fall and create imported inflation
- Might create house price inflation

(c) Supply side policies

(i) Cut benefits

This would reduce government spending and create an incentive to work. Therefore, less people would claim benefit and those people would also become taxpayers increasing tax revenues.

Evaluation

- Could widen gaps between rich and poor
- Workers need to have jobs to go to
- May de-motivate the unemployed

(ii) Cut taxes, e.g. income tax, corporation tax

Cutting income tax would create an incentive to work and gets people off benefits. Cutting corporation tax creates an incentive for businesses to invest and expand creating more jobs. The net result would be that tax revenues rise and benefit payments fall reducing the deficit.

Evaluation

Public spending and taxation

- Could widen gaps between rich and poor
- Workers need to have jobs to go to
- Corporation tax cuts might not be re-invested. They could just be spent on increased dividend payments or bonuses for directors.

<u>(iii) Education and training</u>

This would get people off benefits and into work therefore reducing the deficit.

<u>Evaluation</u>

- May have to raise taxes to pay for it
- Workers need to have jobs to go to
- Time lag
- Quality of courses

Poverty and inequality in developed and developing countries

13

13.1 Absolute and relative poverty

Absolute poverty – this means an individual does not have the basic necessities of life, i.e. food, water, shelter. The World Bank defines absolute poverty as those living on less than $1.90 per day at 2005 GDP PPP. We find this sort of poverty in developing countries.

Relative poverty – this means people living below a certain threshold income in a particular country, e.g. 50% or 60% of median household income. It's the type of poverty we find in developed countries. In the UK and EU the figure is 60%.

13.2 Causes of changes in absolute and relative poverty

(i) Absolute poverty

See sections 14.0 and 15.0 for further detail. Factors include:

- Economic growth
- FDI
- Foreign aid
- Debt relief
- Education and training
- Property rights
- Taxes and benefits
- Government economic policies, e.g. monetary policy
- Fair trade schemes

(ii) Relative poverty

See section 13.11 for further detail.

- Economic growth
- Education and training
- Taxes and benefits
- National minimum wages
- Government economic policies

13.3 Difference between income and wealth inequality

Income inequality – income is a flow concept. Income inequalities means inequalities based on earned and unearned income. Earned income means income on paid employment; unearned income means income based on assets, e.g. interest, dividends, rent.

Wealth inequality - wealth is a stock concept. Wealth inequality means inequalities based on the stock of assets people have, e.g. house, shares, savings, and pensions. In the UK housing is most people's most important asset and it accounts for about 35% of the country's wealth.

13.4 Measurements of inequality – The Lorenz curve

Inequalities in income can be measured using the Lorenz curve. See below:

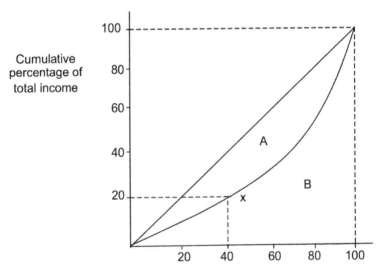

Cumulative percentage of population

The 45° line shows the line of perfect equality, e.g. 20% of the population earns 20% of the total national income. The more the Lorenz curve bows to the right the bigger the inequality, e.g. at point x, 40% of the population only earns about 20% of the total national income. The area between the 45° line and the Lorenz

70

curve (area A) divided by the area of the triangle is called the Gini coefficient [A/(A+B)]. The bigger it is the bigger the inequality. The aim of government policy is to reduce the inequalities using the tax and benefit system and thereby shift the Lorenz curve to the left. At the same time however, it has to take into account the effect on incentives so it wouldn't want perfect equality. The Gini coefficient is measured between 0 and 1. A Gini coefficient of 0 denotes absolute equality; 1 is absolute inequality.

13.5 Causes of income inequalities

Differences in education, training and qualifications - people with higher qualifications are more productive than those with lower qualifications. This means they can earn more money, e.g. doctors vs. cleaners.
Age - older people usually earn more than younger people because they have more experience and have had more time to be promoted. Therefore they can earn more.
Unemployment - those out of work and living on unemployment benefit will have a lot lower standard of living than those in work.
Retirement - those in retirement usually have lower incomes than those still at work because their pensions are usually lower than average wages
Taxes and benefits – tax incentives and levels of benefit will also affect income inequalities. If incentives are high it will encourage people to come off benefit and find work, this will reduce income inequalities. If incentives are low it will widen inequalities. Equally the levels of benefits will effect income inequalities because it affects relative poverty.
Physical and financial wealth - those people with inherited wealth will have income from unearned sources, e.g. dividends and interest. This will cause inequalities in income because they will income from more than one source.

Others:

- The NMW
- Gender
- Discrimination, e.g. race, gender, disability
- Inequality of opportunity – the education system
- Monopsony
- Regional differences in pay

13.6 Causes of wealth inequalities

Different levels of income – the more a person earns the more opportunity they have to save and therefore build up a stock of assets such as a house, savings and shares.
Inheritance - the more a person inherits from previous generations the higher will be their stock of assets.

13.7 Causes of income and wealth inequalities between countries

There are many of these; a suggested list is below. Think about factors effecting international competitiveness (see section 7.4) and factors effecting economic development (see section 14.5):

- Primary product dependency
- Education and training
- Levels of investment, e.g. FDI
- Productivity
- Innovation
- Government economic policies, e.g. taxes and benefits
- Savings ratio
- Corruption
- Lack of natural resources

13.8 Impact of economic change and development on inequality

- Developed countries - in general we would expect, and hope, that further economic development will lead to further reductions in inequality. However, there are wide variations between countries and a lot depends on the tax and benefit system, e.g. in 2012 the Gini coefficient of Denmark was 0.249 but for the UK it was 0.351 (OECD). Income inequality also varies from year to year, and can go up or down.
- Developing countries - in general we would expect economic development to reduce absolute poverty, but increase relative poverty because initially everybody is relatively poor. If we look at China for example 680m people were lifted out of absolute poverty between 1981-2010. However, if we look at relative poverty this increased: in 1984 the Gini coefficient was 0.277, but by 2010 it had risen to 0.421 (World Bank).

Recently there has also been a lot of public disquiet about the impact of globalisation on inequality. The argument has been there have been very large increases in executive pay, but much smaller increases for people at the bottom and in the middle. This has led to widening gaps between rich and poor. There is evidence for this, but it does vary from one country to another.

13.9 Significance of capitalism for inequality

Capitalism inevitably creates inequality in society because it requires incentives for it to work: for the entrepreneur its profit, and for workers its wages. The entrepreneur wants to be rewarded for taking a risk and workers want to be rewarded for their productivity and abilities. The entrepreneur gets paid the most because he's taking the bigger risk, the people who work for him get paid less, but according to ability and what they bring to the firm. If everybody was paid the same the system simply wouldn't work, because there would be a lack of incentive.

Having said this, capitalism is not just about creating inequality. Because of the wealth and tax revenue it creates it can raise living standards for all and lift millions of people out of absolute poverty. Relative poverty is still a problem in developed countries but wages, relatively speaking, are many times higher than they were in the past.

13.10 Consequences of poverty and inequality in developing countries

- **Low savings ratio** – this affects firms ability to invest and expand.
- **Balance of payments problems** – those people on high incomes in the cities may spend it on large volumes of imports because they have a Westernised life style. This in turn can lead to a balance of payments deficit.
- **Lack of entrepreneurship** – the poor will have no capital to start their own business and better themselves because their incomes are not high enough to save.
- **Absolute poverty could remain high** – because of a lack of spending power in the economy and the lack of job creation. Also tax revenues are low, so there is no money to provide merit goods like education and health or develop infrastructure.

- **Capital flight** – in developing countries the very wealthy may transfer their assets to 'safe havens' (see section 14.5)
- **Social problems** – crime, political instability.

13.11 Government policies to redistribute income and reduce poverty

(i) Raise the NMW

Advantages

- Increases incentive to work so it gets people off benefits. Wages are higher than benefits therefore it narrows income differentials between rich and poor.
- Lower wage earners get higher salaries.
- Increases consumer spending and creates a multiplier effect. This reduces unemployment and increases tax revenues. These both benefit the poor.
- Encourages firms to invest more therefore it makes UK firms more competitive. This should reduce unemployment benefiting the poor.

Disadvantages

- May lead to higher costs therefore firms make people redundant. This could make the poor worse off.
- Doesn't help those who are unemployed. It only helps those with a job - therefore it may not really reduce poverty that much.
- Many of the people it helps are working mums or young people living at home - therefore it benefits both the rich and poor.
- Higher income earners may seek to re-establish pay differentials - therefore the effect of the NMW is cancelled out.

(ii) Increase benefits e.g. unemployment benefit, housing benefit

Advantages

- Reduces income inequalities

- Increases spending power of the poor – therefore it creates a multiplier effect and may create more job opportunities and higher tax revenues. These both benefit the poor.

Disadvantages

- May mean taxes have to rise – therefore it creates a disincentive to create wealth. In the long run this might mean slower economic growth, less jobs and lower tax revenues. None of this would benefit the poor.
- Opportunity cost – it may mean less government spending on other public services, e.g. schools and hospitals. This would mean the poor are worse off in the long run.
- It may create a disincentive to work. Therefore the poor prefer to stay on benefit and the gap between rich and poor increases.

(iii) Increase progressive taxes e.g. income tax, corporation tax

Advantages

- Increases tax revenues – therefore government can spend more on benefits and public services reducing income inequalities.
- More public spending by the government creates a multiplier effect, which in turn creates more jobs benefiting the poor.

Disadvantages

- Increasing income tax acts as a disincentive to work – therefore productivity is lower and UK firms become less competitive which might lead to a loss of jobs.
- Increasing corporation tax acts as a disincentive for wealth creators – therefore stifles creativity and innovation. This could lead to lower economic growth in the long run and therefore lower tax revenues and fewer jobs.
- May just increase tax evasion and avoidance so doesn't have any real impact on tax revenues, e.g. Google, Amazon, Starbucks.

(iv) Decrease income tax

Advantages

- Increases incentive to work – therefore encourages people to get jobs and move off benefits reducing income differentials
- Increases the incentive to work harder – therefore raises productivity. In the long-run, UK firms should become more competitive and therefore job security, salaries and number of jobs should increase.
- Increases disposable incomes – therefore consumption increases and creates a multiplier effect, which creates jobs, higher incomes and higher tax revenue.

Disadvantages

- Increases gaps between rich and poor – because it raises the disposable income of the rich more than the disposable income of the poor.
- May reduce tax revenues in the long run – therefore there is less money available for government spending. This could lead to increased gaps between rich and poor in the long run.
- Tax cuts may be saved not spent. Therefore we don't get the multiplier effect expected. If the rich invest this money well it could lead to increased gaps between rich and poor.

(v) Decrease corporation tax

Advantages

- Increases the incentive of wealth creators to start new businesses – therefore it creates more jobs and helps the poor.
- Increases profitability of firms – this means they have more to invest which makes them more competitive and creates more jobs.
- Easier to attract FDI – therefore creates more jobs

Disadvantages

- Reduced corporation tax may mean bigger dividends for shareholders not increased investment.

76

Poverty and inequality

- May mean reduced tax revenues in the long run.

<u>(vi) Switch from indirect tax to direct tax</u> i.e. reduce VAT and raise income tax

<u>Advantages</u>

- VAT is a regressive tax, income tax is a progressive tax therefore switching from one to the other puts less of a tax burden on the poor reducing income inequalities.

<u>Disadvantages</u>

- It could decrease incentives to work – this would affect productivity and competitiveness. In the long run, it could mean a loss of jobs and therefore the poor would be worse off.
- It may decrease incentives for entrepreneurs. This could affect jobs and GDP in the long-run and the poor would be worse off.
- It may reduce tax revenues in the future if GDP slows down – therefore the poor would be worse off.

<u>(vii) Have more bands in income tax at lower levels</u>

By adding extra bands at lower levels it means the poor will pay less tax and it will increase their disposable income, e.g. restore the 10% tax band on the first £2,000 of taxable income abolished in 2008.

<u>Advantages</u>

- Increases the disposable income of the poor
- Creates an incentive for those on low incomes to get jobs and stay off benefits
- Reduces government spending on benefits and therefore means there is more to spend on other public services, e.g. education, health

<u>Disadvantages</u>

- Reduces tax revenues – therefore may affect public spending. This could increase income inequalities.

- May contribute to a budget deficit – therefore could increase government borrowing.

(viii) Others

- Training and education
- Measures to reduce geographical immobility
- Measures to improve healthcare

13.12 Means tested benefits and universal benefits

Means tested benefits – these are benefits that are assessed according to income. Most benefits are of this type. The main problem is the take-up rate is only about 80%.
Universal benefits – these are benefits available to anyone regardless of income, e.g. child benefit, pensions

13.13 Impact of immigration on income inequalities

This is something not directly on the syllabus but is probably worth thinking about as it has been a hot topic in recent years.

Advantages

- New migrants contribute to GDP and help the economy to grow – therefore tax revenues are higher and the government has more money to spend on merit goods and benefits. This will help to reduce income inequalities.
- New migrants help to keep the labour market competitive – therefore UK firms can keep costs low and grow. This creates more jobs helping the poor.

Disadvantages

- Migrants provide competition for UK workers so they might displace UK workers from their jobs creating unemployment. This would widen inequalities.
- Migrants often have lower expectations of wages – therefore they might help to keep wages low and undermine the ability of unions to get higher wages. This would widen income inequalities.

Poverty and inequality

- Migrants might end up working in the hidden economy – therefore the UK develops a dual labour market, which keeps wages low.
- Migrants and their families put added pressure on public services e.g. education and health. Without an increase in taxation this could mean less resources being focused on poorer families and therefore widening income inequalities.

Emerging and developing economies

14

14.1 Economic growth and economic development

Economic growth – means an increase in the productive capacity of the economy. It's measured by increases in real GDP.
Economic development – means an improvement in living standards and economic welfare over time. The most common measure used is the Human Development Index (HDI).

14.2 Classification/characteristics of countries

Developed countries – also known as First World Countries or Most Developed Countries (MDC's) have the following characteristics:

- Tend to be thought of as Western
- Many have entered a phase of de-industrialisation and have developed the service sector of their economies in response.
- High GDP per head
- High levels of education and health care
- High productivity and investment
- Non-corrupt democratically elected governments

In the post-war period Hong Kong, Singapore and South Korea have raised their incomes to the point where they are regarded as developed countries. A number of other countries are not far behind. These sorts of countries are known as Newly Industrialised Countries/Economies (NIC's/NIE's)

Developing countries - also known as Third World Countries or Less Developed Countries (LDC's) have the following characteristics:

- Tend to be located in Africa, South America and Asia
- Low incomes and GDP per head
- Tend to be agriculture or subsistence based economy's. Export earnings are often dependent on primary products and industrial/manufacturing sector is small.

- Poor financial infrastructure
- Poor healthcare, education and communication infrastructure
- High unemployment and underemployment
- Low productivity and investment
- High birth rates and death rates
- Often led by corrupt, non-democratically elected governments

14.3 Measures of development – The Human Development Index (HDI)

The HDI is a measure of the quality of life constructed by the United Nations Development Programme. It's based on three main indicators:

- Life expectancy at birth.
- Educational attainment – this is composed of two figures: mean years schooling and expected years schooling (primary, secondary and tertiary).
- GNI per head at purchasing power parity (PPP).

It's based on the belief that there are three key aspects to human development: resources, knowledge on how to use those resources, and a reasonable life span in which to make use of those resources. Purchasing power parity means using an exchange rate based on the cost of a basket of goods, rather than on the official exchange rate.

The HDI is a number between 0 to 1 and the countries are grouped in quartiles: very high, high, medium and low.

(i) Examples

Country	Development	HDI Rank	HDI Value	Life Expectancy	Mean Years Schooling	GNI per capita ($)
UK	Very High	14	0.907	80.7	13.1	39,267
France	Very High	22	0.888	82.2	11.1	38,056
Brazil	High	75	0.755	74.5	7.7	15,175
China	High	90	0.727	75.8	7.5	12,547
South Africa	Medium	116	0.666	57.4	9.9	12,122
Vietnam	Medium	116	0.666	75.8	7.5	5,092
Angola	Low	149	0.532	52.3	4.7	6,822
Senegal	Low	170	0.466	66.5	2.5	2,188

(ii) Advantages

Uses reliable and fairly easy to obtain indicators – life expectancy, educational attainment and real GDP are indicators most governments can obtain the figures for fairly easily.
Indicators chosen are cheap and easy to collect – this minimises the costs for poorer countries and means they are more likely to provide them.
Use of education and health can be used to assess the impact of government policies – this is important not only for developing countries but developed countries as well.
Doesn't just focus on income per capita – includes life expectancy and educational standards as well so gives a broader view of a country's development.

(iii) Limitations

Omits other important dimensions of development – for example, housing quality, pollution, unemployment, education quality, crime rates, inflation.
Gives equal weighting to all three indices – in calculation of the HDI each of the indices is given the same weight. This doesn't seem fair. One might have expected more weight to be given to increases in real GDP.
Distance between ranks is more important than ranks in themselves – understanding the HDI requires careful evaluation. If the data is compressed one country may be well below another in terms of rank but the distance in terms of the HDI may be small.
Civil war, health issues, political instability – some countries may be well down the list because of civil war, public health issues like HIV/ AIDS or because of political instability. This is particularly true of countries in Africa and sub-Saharan Africa. This will skew the data.
Omits regional differences – the HDI is calculated for the whole country. It doesn't show what's happening in different regions of that country.
Ignores social and environmental costs of development – e.g. crime, family breakdown, pollution.
Educational attainment – doesn't tell us about quality of schooling.

14.4 Other measures of development

Emerging and developing economies

Other measures of development that are currently used are:

- Percentage of adult male labour in agriculture
- Combined primary and secondary school enrolment figures
- Access to clean water, housing, infant mortality
- Energy consumption per head
- Access to mobile phones per thousand of the population

14.5 Factors influencing growth and development

(i) Primary product dependency

This is a separate topic in itself - see section 14.6.

(ii) Poor infrastructure

This means poor road, rail and air links, but also a lack of water and energy supplies, and a communications infrastructure. Poor road and rail links makes it difficult to move goods and raw materials around the country increasing costs. A lack of water and energy supplies means it's difficult to keep factories running all day and effects productivity. A lack of communications infrastructure, such as telephone and internet services, effect communication with customers and suppliers. In total it deters foreign investment and growth, e.g. India ranked 87th in infrastructure in the World Economic Forum's Global Competitiveness Index (2014)

Evaluation

- Foreign aid can be used to improve and maintain infrastructure
- Foreign investors can be persuaded to improve infrastructure where a developing country has valuable raw materials and/or represents a new market for foreign firms, e.g. Chinese investment in Africa was $3.4bn in 2013, and for many years has been used for a range of projects including roads, rail and power plants.

(iii) Education and skills

Education standards effect the human capital of the population. If it's low, productivity will be low, because people won't have the skills to do more complicated jobs. It means a country can't move from an agriculture, or subsistence based economy, to one based on manufacturing and services, e.g. the average years schooling of an adult in Angola is only 4.7 (2014). It also deters foreign investment.

Evaluation

- Education and skills can be improved fairly quickly as long as the political will for change is there, e.g. Oportunidades programme in Mexico, Bolsa Familia in Brazil.
- Foreign aid can also be used to improve education standards.

(iv) Savings gap

The level of savings affects how much money the banks can lend and therefore how much investment takes place. This in turn affects jobs, growth and incomes. It also affects the ability of a country to diversify its economy and expand its industrial/manufacturing sector. In LDC's savings tend to be low because of low incomes, capital flight and people don't trust the banking system, e.g. China's gross national savings are about 50% of GDP but in Uganda it's only about 16% (2013). We can see the importance of the savings gap in the Harrod-Domar model (see section 15.1).

Evaluation

- Savings gap can be filled by FDI, aid or debt cancellation, e.g. FDI flows to Africa in 2014 were about $60bn

(v) Debt

Government debt can become an obstacle to growth because it creates a climate of uncertainty and risk. Paying off the loans means that less can be spent on education and infrastructure, for example, so the economy suffers. Investors might also think the government might have to raise taxes to pay for the debt and therefore growth in the local economy will be low. There is also the problem of a cycle of debt, where interest payments are so high the government can never really pay the capital off.

Evaluation

- Debt cancellation can ease the problem of external debt, e.g. in 2005 the World Bank, IMF and African Development Fund jointly wrote off $40bn of debt from the 18 most Heavily Indebted Poor Countries (HIPC)
- Government debt varies from one country to another and may only be a problem for the very poorest countries, e.g. in Nigeria it was 19% of GDP in 2012, but in Sudan 89% (CIA Factbook).

(vi) Corruption & poor governance

Corruption affects investment in public services and incentives to work. Corrupt governments will take tax revenues themselves rather than investing it in health, education and infrastructure. Equally people will have a disincentive to work hard or start their own business if they think the government will take their money. Corruption also means that individuals have an incentive to get a good government job rather being productive in the economy. Overall it slows growth, e.g. the African Union estimates corruption costs their countries about 25% of their combined national income.

Poor governance works somewhat in the same way. Instead of taxes or aid being used to build up infrastructure and human capital, it may just be used to buy weapons and keep the government in power, e.g. Robert Mugabe in Zimbabwe.

Evaluation

- The problem of corruption varies from one country to another, e.g. Chile ranks 21 on the Global Corruption Perception Index but Angola is 106
- There are some countries where corruption is a problem but growth has still been strong, e.g. China, India.

(vii) Demographic factors

In general, countries with rapidly growing populations and high birth rates are poor ones, e.g. Angola had a birth rate of 6.08 in 2014 and Senegal 5.09 (World Bank). This is because if the population is growing faster than GDP, then GDP per head will be falling. It also puts a strain on education and healthcare because more government spending has to be devoted to those areas. Finally, it could mean higher unemployment later on if the economy is not growing fast enough to provide people with jobs.

Evaluation

- Larger supply of labour will keep wages low making a country attractive for FDI.
- Creates young entrepreneurial workforce.
- Dependency ratio may fall later on, so less needs to be spent on education and healthcare.
- More people means more output, so per capita incomes may rise later.

(viii) Capital flight

This means wealthy individuals, and firms, withdrawing their capital from a country and depositing it, or buying assets, in safer countries, e.g. in Europe, America. This may happen in response to a financial crisis or political instability.

It can effect economic growth and development because it effects investment, jobs and the foreign currency gap.

(ix) Foreign currency gap

This means having insufficient foreign exchange in order to promote higher economic growth, e.g. purchase of capital goods, raw materials, and components. It can happen because of primary product dependency, an over-reliance on imports and capital flight. The problem can be solved by diversifying the economy, foreign aid and FDI.

(x) Access to credit

This effects entrepreneurial activity. In many developing countries the banking system is limited, so there is an inevitable knock-on effect to business activity. Micro-finance schemes are an attempt to get around the problem. See section 15.2 (vi).

(xi) Absence of property rights

Emerging and developing economies

Property rights create incentives to use assets in their most efficient way, e.g. land, property, intellect. The absence of them leads to 'dead capital' (Hernando De Soto). A significant problem in developing countries is that it's often difficult to establish who has legal title over what, particularly land and property. In the case of diamond mining, for example, in the Central African Republic, it has led to miners being exploited because they can't establish legal ownership of their land.

If we take Taiwan as a counter example, land reform in the 1950's, giving private property rights to farmers, led to growing agricultural yields because farmers had a greater incentive to produce, and it also meant land could be put to other use, e.g. building a factory. Taiwan is now of course a developed country.

(xii) Others

- Civil wars
- AIDS/disease - the AIDS infection rate in South Africa is about 19% (2015)
- Lack of natural resources

14.6 Primary product dependency

This means an economy being largely dependent on the export of a few primary products, e.g. tin, copper, cocoa, rubber.

(i) Examples

These are the percentage of total exports for some African countries in 2014 (UN Comtrade):

- Ghana: 26% gold, 23% oil, 22% cocoa
- Kenya: 16% tea, 12% horticulture
- Nigeria: 74% oil, 13% gas
- Tanzania: 21% gold
- Uganda: 20% coffee
- Zambia: 77% copper
- Angola: 96% oil

(ii) Problems

- **Price fluctuations** – commodities tend to have inelastic supply and demand creating price fluctuations, which creates uncertainty in revenues and profits for producers. This makes jobs insecure and makes it difficult for firms to plan ahead and invest.
- **Value added is low** – commodities tend to be low priced compared to the eventual end product, e.g. coffee beans vs coffee. This means wages and standards of living are low. It also means profits are low and makes diversification less likely because there's less money to invest with.
- **Low income elasticity of demand (YED)** – the Prebisch-Singer hypothesis states that the terms of trade between primary and manufactured goods tend to deteriorate over time (see section 2.3). This leads to problems for the balance of payments and growth.
- **Natural disasters** – 'soft commodities' like agricultural products are severely affected by extreme weather like hurricanes, droughts and tsunamis.
- **Fluctuations in foreign currency earnings** – since there can be large price changes from one year to the next. This can constrain the import of capital goods and therefore development.
- **Protectionism by developed countries** – e.g. EU's Common Agricultural Policy (CAP) means developing countries have to pay a tariff to export their goods to the EU.
- **External costs** – e.g. mining – environmental damage and effect on landscape; agriculture – deforestation, environmental impact.

(iii) Evaluation

- **LDC's may have a comparative advantage in primary products** – therefore you could say they should develop in the area where they are strongest.
- **Some countries have developed on the basis of their primary products** – e.g. Saudi Arabia, Kuwait – oil; Botswana – diamonds. These industries have provided growth, jobs and tax revenue which the government can then use to build schools, hospitals and infrastructure making the economy stronger. If it uses the money well it can diversify its economy and continue growing.

- **Demand may be income elastic** - e.g. gold – Ghana; diamonds – Botswana; oil – Nigeria. That means as world income grows, demand will increase.
- **Primary products rose steeply in price between 2000-2008 while prices for manufactured goods was falling** – with the continuing development of the BRIC countries and change in diets in China and India some economists would say primary product prices are set to remain high for some time.

Strategies influencing growth and development

15

15.1 Models/theories of growth and development

Harrod-Domar model – this theory of economic development emphasises the importance of investment, savings and technological change to increase growth. Increased investment pushes the PPF out, as does the introduction of new technologically advanced capital. If governments can increase the capital output ratio this will therefore create economic growth and development. According to this model the reason why economies remain undeveloped is because of a lack of savings. Without savings there are no funds for investment and without investment development can't take place. It provides a good argument for FDI and foreign aid to close the savings gap.
Rostow's 5 stages of development – Rostow said that economies went through 5 stages:

- The traditional society where most people live on the land and agriculture is the main industry.
- The transition stage in which manufacturing has begun to develop and savings are beginning to rise to about 15-20% of national income.
- The take-off stage in which investment increases rapidly and the country begins to use its resources and infrastructure to create sustained economic growth.
- The drive to maturity, when both the manufacturing and service sectors expand production.
- The stage of mass consumption, the economy has finally 'made it' and is at the level of developed countries.

For Rostow, savings was again the key element to development. It's what gets an economy from stages 3 to 4.
Lewis 2-sector model – Lewis saw developing economies as being characterised by two sectors, the capitalist industrial sector and the subsistence agriculture sector. According to his theory, development proceeds by the capitalist industrial sector drawing on the cheap labour supply of the subsistence agriculture sector. Wages stay low because of unemployment and underemployment on the land. This means the industrial sector can make large profits that can then be re-invested to expand output and create

yet more jobs that those working on the land can be transferred into. This transfer of labour between agriculture and industry will continue to take place, with no rise in wages, until all the surplus labour on the land has been absorbed. In the mean time the economy would have grown and development would have taken place. It's called a 'structural change model' because it refers to the structure of economies.

Dependency theory – this theory emphasises the role of the historical links between First World and Third World countries. It says the lack of development in LDC's is not so much due to internal conditions in the country, and a lack of savings, but external forces due to their colonial past. The First World countries may have left, but they have continued their domination over the Third World countries by forcing them to specialise in primary production and this primary product dependency has locked them into a cycle of slow growth and development. This situation has been made worse by Western institutions (like the IMF), locking the Third World countries into a cycle of debt ironically to increase their development.

Market liberalisation/neo-classical theory – this theory emphasises the role of the market in promoting development. Protectionism should be reduced and privatisation and deregulation encouraged. In addition FDI should be sought by LDC's to help them develop their economies and infrastructure.

15.2 Ways to promote growth and development in developing countries

There are many of these split into three categories:

- Market orientated
- Interventionist
- Other

Some are explained in detail others are suggested. The policies shown in detail are the ones which have most frequently appeared on the exam in the past.

(a) Market orientated strategies

(i) Trade liberalisation

Strategies influencing growth and development

This means removing barriers to trade, e.g. tariffs, quotas and promoting free trade, e.g. China since the 1980's.

For

- Trade liberalisation can lead to gains from comparative advantage
- Creates jobs and growth – access to larger markets, FDI
- Increased competition can be a good thing for domestic firms – encourages them to be more efficient.
- Access to global markets leads to economies of scale and greater efficiency.
- More attractive for FDI
- Access to global finance – important for investment

Against

- Reducing protectionism could increase unemployment
- Domestic firms can't develop properly because competition is too strong.
- Higher prices for basic necessities
- May widen gaps between rich and poor
- Increases externalities
- Might effect infant industries

(ii) Promotion of FDI

This can be done through reducing corporation tax, government grants and reducing bureaucracy.

For analysis and evaluation see section 11.3

(iii) Microfinance schemes

This means giving small businesses in LDC's access to small loans from local lenders, e.g. SKS Microfinance, India

For

- Should encourage local entrepreneurship and therefore grassroots development of the economy, e.g. start a small shop, expand family farm.

- Helps the poor to increase their incomes so reduces poverty and increases standards of living, e.g. means poor families can afford school fees.
- Should increase growth and reduce unemployment.

Against

- May be difficult to get off the ground because locals don't want to take a risk and get into debt.
- Lack of education may mean locals don't understand what micro-finance loans are and what the terms are.
- Micro-creditors may take advantage of debtors and charge extortionate rates of interest.
- May mean a reduction in other forms of aid for the poor

(iv) Removal of government subsidies

Government subsidies distort market forces and make domestic producers complacent and inefficient. Their removal will help make them more competitive and help the economy grow.

(v) Floating exchange rate systems

This could allow the value of the currency to fall making exports cheaper and imports more expensive thereby encouraging economic growth.

(vi) Privatisation

This should promote efficiency and productivity in what were once nationalised industries. It will also mean more tax revenue for the government because less will be spent on subsidies.

(b) Interventionist strategies

(i) Development of education system/human capital

This means increasing school enrolment at primary, secondary and tertiary levels and increasing training at work. This means building more schools and training more teachers, e.g. Oportunidades is a Mexican government scheme aimed at increasing educational attainment by giving cash payments to poor families in exchange for regular school attendance, health clinic visits and nutritional support. Brazil has a similar scheme called Bolsa Familia.

For

- Improves skill level of the population and increases productivity
- Reduces unemployment – easier for people to find jobs once their skills have improved
- More attractive for FDI
- Improves international competitiveness – raises productivity
- Reduces corruption – a better educated population is less likely to be corrupt.

Against

- Cost - a good education system requires money and developing countries will always struggle with this, e.g. building schools, training teachers
- Parents may not be able to afford school fees
- Time lag – it will take 18 years before full effects are felt
- Corruption - poor governance and corruption has meant money intended for schools has been 'lost' in the system.
- Brain drain – best educated people may just leave the country
- In some countries you could argue that political stability is more important than education. Without it the education system can't be improved.

(ii) Protectionism

Also known as 'import substitution', this means using tariffs, quotas and subsidies for home producers to bring about a long-term improvement in the economy. The aims would be diversification and/or industrialisation.

For

- Protects jobs
- Promotes import substitution - brings about long-term improvement in the balance of payments.

- Protects 'infant industries' – once they are strong enough and have sufficient economies of scale and investment to compete with Western companies import controls can be removed.
- Prevents dumping
- Allows controlled diversification of the economy to take place

Against

- Distorts comparative advantage – therefore resources in the economy not being allocated in the most efficient way
- Protection might make home industries inefficient and unrealistic and therefore once the protection is taken off they can't compete on the world stage.
- Retaliation – other countries may react by restricting your exports
- Reduced consumer choice

(iii) Managed exchange rate

Some countries try to deliberately undervalue their currency in order to make their exports cheaper, e.g. China has done this in the past with the Renimbi. It's also possible to do this the other way round in order to keep import costs down.

(iv) Infrastructure development

For the importance of this see section 14.5 (ii)

(v) Promoting joint ventures with global companies

This is to get around the perceived exploitation by MNC's. The government can insist that if any investment takes place it has to be in joint venture with a local company, e.g. 50:50. This means part of the profits always stay in the country but there is still the transfer of knowledge.

(vi) Buffer stock schemes

These try to even out price fluctuations in commodity markets, e.g. cocoa, coffee. The aim is to make it easier to plan ahead, encourage investment and protect jobs. This was covered in detail in Theme 1.

(c) Other strategies

(i) Aid

Foreign aid can be in the form of grants, loans or for humanitarian reasons (food, medicine). Further, agreements can be between just two countries (bi-lateral) or between many countries (multi-lateral), e.g. Angola received about $230m in total from foreign aid in 2014, Senegal $1.1bn.

For

- Can be used to reduce absolute poverty – food, grain, jobs.
- Fills the savings gap – Harrod-Domar model, Rostow's 5 stages of development.
- Provides funds for infrastructure – therefore creates jobs, a multiplier effect and growth.
- Improves human capital – aid can be used to improve education and the health system.
- Helps to develop sectoral development – away from agricultural and primary product dependency.

Against

- Much aid has been wasted on prestige projects such as dams rather than grass roots projects such as schools. LDC governments have been more concerned with their own prestige rather than doing the practical long-term thing.
- Aid could be wasted on arms and keeping the present government in power rather than tackling economic problems.
- Corruption has meant much foreign aid has been lost in the system. Local politicians have benefited but the poor haven't.
- Aid payments have sometimes been tied to a commitment to buy goods from the donor country. This has led to them paying higher prices than if they had shopped around.

Strategies influencing growth and development

- Foreign aid in the form of subsidised food or goods could just increase dependency in the long run. In the short-run it decreases prices for local farmers anyway.
- Loans have to be repaid with interest. This just builds up debts and makes the situation worse.

(ii) Debt relief

This means Western countries and big financial institutions such as the IMF cancelling and/or rescheduling their debts with developing countries, e.g. the joint World Bank-IMF Heavily Indebted Poor Countries Initiative (HIPC). To date 36 countries, 30 of them in Africa, have benefited from about $75bn of cancelled debt from this scheme.

For

- Helps to reduce absolute poverty – instead of repaying debt the government will have more money to spend on health, education and infrastructure and building the country's future.
- Means there is more foreign currency to buy imported capital goods and consumer goods from the developed countries.
- Helps to reduce savings gap – instead of government tax receipts being spent on debt repayment it will be deposited in banks where it can be lent out.
- Might help to conserve the environment, e.g. 'debt for nature swaps'.

Against

- May just encourage developing countries to get into debt all over again because they think eventually it will be cancelled.
- May just encourage dependency on the West.
- Corruption – government officials benefit not the economy.
- Unless there are conditions no guarantee money will be spent in the right way, e.g. wasted on defence spending, prestige projects.
- Banks in developed countries suffer losses – knock-on effects to jobs, dividends and growth in the West.

Strategies influencing growth and development

(iii) Development of tourism

Many LDC's have increasingly developed tourism as a way of developing their economies. And for some countries it may be the main product that they have to sell, e.g. tourism is about 69% of the exports of The Bahamas (2014).

For

- Creates jobs – tourism is labour intensive rather than capital intensive so it creates lots of jobs, e.g. hotel staff, kitchen staff, tour guides, transport.
- Increases growth – via increased consumption and the multiplier
- Increases incomes and standards of living – reduces unemployment and provides higher wages than agriculture, fishing
- Improves infrastructure – airports, roads need to be built
- Increases tax revenues
- Diversifies the economy – spreads risk and provides jobs in a different sector of the economy.

Against

- Tourists tend to demand goods that have to be imported this creates leakages from the circular flow of income. The net effect on the economy may therefore be not that great.
- Employment may only be seasonal
- Demand for tourism is income elastic so when Western countries have a recession demand falls – demand is unstable.
- May cause significant externalities, e.g., pollution, litter, damage to the environment.
- Weakens local culture and makes it more Western.

(iv) Fair trade schemes

This means giving producers in LDC's a fair price for their products. They get this in return for meeting particular labour and production standards. Examples include coffee, cocoa, cotton, wine and clothes.

For

- Producers receive a higher price for their products so it improves their living standard.
- The fair trade co-operative has funds available for local social projects, e.g. education, health, clean water, infrastructure.
- Easier for producers to plan ahead - because there are smaller price fluctuations.
- Producers will find it easier to diversify because their income is more stable.

Against

- Lack of education and remoteness may mean that many small producers are unaware of the schemes.
- Membership fees are required to join the schemes and to stay part of them.
- Non-fair trade producers may see a fall in demand for their products.
- Some people say it's just a way to help retailers and consumers in the developed world feel better and as if they are doing something to help small producers in the developing countries. In reality the affects are minimal.

(v) Development of agriculture

This means policies to make the agricultural sector in developing countries more efficient. It would include policies such as:

- Land reform
- Disease control
- Provision of microfinance and credit for farmers
- World commodity agreements and buffer stock schemes to stabilise agricultural prices.

For

- Many developing countries have a comparative advantage in agriculture so it's developing their economies where they are strongest.
- Should make agriculture more efficient and increase food production benefiting the poor.

Strategies influencing growth and development

- Should remove risk from the agricultural sector encouraging investment and growth.
- Should increase tax revenues – government can use this to build schools, hospitals and in time diversify the economy.
- Some agricultural products have a high YED, e.g. Peru – asparagus; Chile – wine, blueberries. They are not necessarily always low value items.
- Some developed countries have a large volume of exports from food, e.g. France - 14% (2013)

Against

- Danger of developing primary product dependency and all the problems associated with it – low value added content, price fluctuations.
- External costs – deforestation, environmental damage of 'agri-businesses'. Might be better to use intermediate technology associated with micro-finance projects and small producers.
- Falling terms of trade – Prebisch-Singer hypothesis.
- Buffer stock systems and price stability agreements have a bad track record – most fail in the end.

(vi) Industrialisation – development of manufacturing

Lewis and other economists have argued the only effective route to economic development is via a thorough going industrialisation, e.g. China since the 1980's.

For

- Excess labour on the land can be used to provide cheap labour for the factories in urban areas and the profits made thereof can be used to re-invest and create a virtuous circle of growth.
- Reform of agriculture means more workers can be released for the urban areas and as more people find employment in factories wages will rise raising living standards.
- Improves savings ratio as incomes rise – banks will then have more money to lend out for investment.

- Attracts in FDI – MNC's can take advantage of cheap labour.

Against

- Not all profits are re-invested by MNC's - much can leak out of the country, e.g. repatriated profits, dividends.
- New investment can create unemployment as well as employment – workers come from the land looking for jobs but can't find one. The result is slums.
- Industrialisation increases gaps between rich and poor.
- Small scale farming may be better at limiting social and environmental costs
- Opportunity costs of industrialisation – less land to grow food.

(vii) Development of primary industries

There are examples of countries developing on the basis of their primary industries. For details see section 14.6

15.3 Role of international finance institutions and NGO's in promoting growth and development

The three big international finance institutions connected with economic development are:

(i) The International Monetary Fund (IMF)

This was established to promote exchange rate stability and to provide short–term loans to sort out balance of payments problems. More recently it has become a source of funds to developing countries to provide short-term stabilisation after/during an economic crisis, e.g. Asian Financial Crisis (1997). It's funded by member countries based on their GDP. In 2006 it was given the new role of multi-lateral surveillance of the global economy.

Evaluation

- Loans have been tied to painful conditions such as cuts in public spending and control of monetary growth. This has caused as many problems as it has solved.

- Loans just mean developing countries get further into debt and have to spend more scarce resources servicing the debt creating a cycle of poverty.

(ii) World Bank

The proper name for the World Bank is the International Bank of Reconstruction and Development (IBRD). It provides funds for developing countries that stimulate long-term growth, e.g. infrastructure, industry, education, health.

Evaluation

- Loans come with conditions that are not necessarily helpful, e.g. many countries have been forced to implement radical supply-side policies such as privatisation, trade liberalisation and cuts in public spending to reduce budget deficits. China, however, has shown where state institutions have remained rapid growth has been possible.
- Loans have been spent on 'prestige projects' not projects that are likely to promote long-term economic growth.
- Loans just create more debt and a cycle of debt that the developing countries can't escape.

(iii) World Trade Organisation (WTO)

This promotes free trade and settles trade disputes. The main criticism is that free trade doesn't necessarily equal fair trade and any agreements reached under the WTO are almost bound to favour the developed countries not the developing ones.

(iv) Non-governmental organisations (NGO's)

These are organisations that are not associated either with governments or with firms in the private sector. Usually they are either charities or pressure groups, e.g. Oxfam, Cafod. They are often associated with either health or education projects.

Benefits

- Can provide effective relief in key areas – health and education.

Strategies influencing growth and development

- Can act as pressure groups on governments and campaign for change thereby reducing poverty.

Limitations

- The help they can provide will always be limited. No number of charities can do what a government could do, e.g. provide a fully funded NHS service

The financial sector

16

<u>16.1 The role of financial markets</u>

- To facilitate saving - for individuals and firms.
- To lend to businesses and individuals - e.g. loans, mortgages, overdrafts.
- To facilitate the exchange of goods and services - e.g. debit cards, credit cards, cheques, ATMs
- To provide forward markets in currencies and commodities - this means buying or selling currencies and commodities in advance. The idea is to reduce the risk of price fluctuations. However, it can also be used to speculate on price movements.
- To provide a market for equities - equities are shares in companies listed on the stock exchange. The stock market provides a place where firms can issue shares and raise finance for expansion; it's also the place where shares can be traded with other investors.

<u>16.2 Market failure in the financial sector</u>

Asymmetric information - this means unequal information between buyers and sellers. It happens because financial products have become increasingly complex. It can happen between financial institutions or between financial institutions and clients, e.g. a mortgage broker selling a client a mortgage which pays him the highest commission, but isn't the best product for the client.
Externalities - these are the effects on third parties who weren't directly involved in the financial transaction, e.g. the cost to UK taxpayers of solving the financial crisis: about £120bn.
Moral hazard - this means people and financial institutions acting in their own interest knowing that others are likely to bear the risk, e.g. risky trades, excessive lending.
Speculation and market bubbles - market bubbles occur when assets are excessively overvalued and the price collapses, e.g. housing, shares. It's an old Wall Street saying that markets are ruled by fear and greed.
Market rigging - this means collusion between individuals or institutions to fix prices. Two recent examples have been the Libor scandal involving several banks, including Barclays and UBS; the

other was a foreign exchange scandal, involving many banks, including HSBC and Deutsche Bank.

<u>16.3 Role of central banks</u>

Implementation of monetary policy - this includes setting interest rates and control of the money supply, e.g. QE.
Banker to the government - most central banks act as banker to the government. This is where the government keeps their accounts.
Banker to the banks - the central bank acts as a banker to the commercial banks. It often requires them to hold a reserve balance with them to act as a safeguard on the banking system. It also acts as 'lender of last resort' if a bank gets into trouble.
Role in regulation of the banking industry - the central bank attempts to provide a framework in which the banking industry operates. For example, following the financial crisis, the Bank of England set up the Prudential Regulation Authority (PRA) in 2012. Its two main functions are to promote safety and soundness in the banking system, and to facilitate effective competition.

External shocks and problems facing policy makers

17

17.1 External shocks

By external shocks we mean major disruptions to the global economy. They can happen either be on the demand side or supply side:

(i) Supply-side shocks

- War
- Natural disasters, e.g. hurricane, tsunami
- Sudden disruption to the supply of oil

These kinds of events move supply sharply to the left as firms feel uncertain about the future and it may also mean that production facilities have been destroyed.

(ii) Demand side shocks

- Sudden changes in interest rates
- Financial crisis - credit crunch

These affect consumer confidence. Consumers cut back spending because they want to save their money and wait and see how the situation develops. Businesses cut back investment for the same reason, and also because they think consumption will fall.

The policy response varies from situation to situation, but the objective is to restore business and consumer confidence, e.g. after the financial crisis of 2008, the UK government slashed interest rates and bailed out the banks.

17.2 Problems facing policy makers

Inaccurate information - information can be inaccurate because it's out-of- date, estimated or just difficult to collect. This can lead to the wrong policies being pursued, although governments obviously try to minimise it. It's worth remembering that because some economics numbers are very small, even small differences in actual figures compared to estimates, can make big differences in the end, e.g. UK economic growth in 2016 is forecast to be 1.6%, but 0.2% of 1.6% is a difference of 12.5%. This could have a big effect on tax receipts, for example.

Risks and uncertainties - many decisions are finely balanced and it's not easy to predict the outcome, e.g. Brexit. This can lead to the wrong course of action, so policy makers need to have alternatives if it seems their decision is not going according to plan.

Inability to control external shocks - no one can control all factors and external shocks can come from nowhere, e.g. financial crisis. Having said this, some people had predicted the financial crisis because of light-touch regulation.

Appendix 1 - UK economy key statistics 2017-18

(1) Income tax

- There are three bands for income tax: basic rate is 20%, higher rate is 40% and the additional rate is 45%. The additional rate applies to income over £150,000.
- Personal allowance is £11,500 this year and the government plans for this to rise to £12,500 by 2020
- Higher rate tax threshold is £45,000
- The government plans to increase the threshold for higher rate tax payers to £50,000 by 2020.
- Median income in UK is £26,300. About 800,000 earn more than £100,000.

(2) VAT

- Labour government temporarily reduced VAT to 15% in 2009 in reaction to financial crisis
- Coalition government (Conservative-LibDems) increased it to 17.5% again in 2010
- Coalition government further increased it to 20% in 2011/12 where it has remained

(3) Corporation tax

Main corporation tax rate – profits over £300,000

2011-12: 26%
2012-13: 24%
2013-14: 23%
2014-15: 21%
2015-16: 20%
2016-17: 20%
2017-18: 19%

- The government plans to cut the main corporation tax rate to 17% by 2020
- Patent box – this is a tax relief introduced in 2013. Companies with patents can put them in a "patent box" and only pay 10% corporation tax on the profits they generate. This is to incentivise innovation.

UK economy key statistics

- Research and development (R&D) tax credits – these were introduced in 2000 and have the effect of reducing a firm's corporation tax liability. In 2015 the government once again increased their generosity.

(4) Benefits cap

- Coalition government introduced it in 2013.
- It was set at £26,000 for couples or single parents with children, and £18,500 for single people
- From 2016 the benefit cap was cut to £20,000 nationally for couples or single parents with children, and £23,000 in London. For single people the benefit cap was cut to £13,400 nationally and £15,400 in London.

(5) Quantitative easing/monetary policy

- Total QE has been £375bn since 2009
- Project Merlin (2011) – agreement between banks and government to increase lending to small/medium sized business
- Funding for Lending Scheme (FLS) [2012] – provides cheaper funding to banks that increase loans to households and businesses
- "Forward guidance" – introduced by Mark Carney in August 2013. It means the BOE giving guidance in advance about future monetary policy, e.g. BOE base rate.

(6) National Minimum Wage/National Living Wage (2017)

NMW

- Under 18: £4.05
- 18-20: £5.60
- 21-24: £7.05

National Living Wage (25+): £7.50

(7) Budget statistics 2017-18: Treasury

Forecast government spending = £802bn

Welfare = £245bn (31%)
Health = £149bn (19%)
Education = £102bn (13%)
Debt interest = £46bn
Public order & safety = £34bn

Forecast government tax receipts = £744bn

Income tax = £175bn (24%)
VAT = £143bn (19%)
National insurance = £130bn (17%)
Excise duty = £48bn
Corporation tax = £52bn (7%)

Forecast deficit = £58bn

Index

Printed in Great Britain
by Amazon